Introduction

We are now living in a rapidly changing world, which seems to be moving at an exponential rate. An ineffable amount of changes just within the past 150 years have created a different world now to one that was known before. Some changes have been beneficial, some catastrophic and some things haven't changed at all. This is the way the world works. Yet it is seen more and more by an ever increasing mass of people that something just isn't quite right. Some of these changes are so blatant that none could miss it, even if their eyes were closed. On the other hand some changes are so subtle that they pass before our eyes unnoticed like the air we breathe. It is about one of these subtle changes on which this piece of work is going to focus.

What is that subtle change that affects our lives so deeply yet we are unaware of it? The answer lies in a word.

What we are presented with before us is but one simple word. That's right; one word. A word so common, so ubiquitous that one would be surprised at the mischief, confusion and debate it has caused. It is a word that has evolved, over thousands of years, corrupted from its original form, undergoing a transformation that would be analogous to a single seed becoming a mighty forest. Unlike many parts of our language which wither away and are forgotten in antiquity, or others that enter and leave our language in but a single generation, this slippery little word continues with us like a chameleon adapting itself to a hostile environment.

So what is this pernicious little word that has created such pandemonium? Laughingly it is but the ridiculously commonplace word "person." That's it!

One may even ask the question, "why would a paper need to be written on such a seemingly banal and insipid part of our language?" It must be one of the most commonly used words in the English language and at the same time most misunderstood. Yet it is because it is a part of our language, a part which affects everyone in the English speaking world, that it is our duty that it must be questioned, analysed and understood.

A resurfacing of the nature of this word is now being contested in many areas, none more so than in the area of law, and if there is one area of life that touches the lives of everyone to a greater or lesser extent, it is that of the Law. Innocent people are convicted wrongly on the use of this word. It restricts our lives covertly in so many ways, and yet we are ignorant of this. Certain people in power abuse this ignorance of the word's meaning and use it to their advantage causing hardship and distress to the common man or woman.

So does it not behove us to look more closely at this problematic little part of our everyday speech. Can we now dare to put an end to this bewilderment that affects all men and women alike? Can clarity be achieved? Because what it comes down to is one simple question "Is a human being a person"

It is the aim of this work to provide clarification on this word; to elucidate its encroachment into some of the more important spheres of our lives and what the upshot of this is to us, the people. This will be achieved by firstly looking into the common definition, combined with the etymology and usage of the word "person." Then we will look at how this word is used in the area of law, delving into the world of "legal persons," and the idea of a "legal personality." In the final part we will look more closely into the laws of this country and the interpretation of our contentious little friend or foe, for it has yet to be decided whether it is an ally or the enemy, or neither or both.

A little disclaimer must be added here. To avoid confusion I will be using the word man to avoid the commonly used word "person." There are no sexist connotations to this, as when I write man, I mean man, woman, child, boy, girl and human being. Do not be offended by the usage of the word man it is simply a tool to avoid any misunderstanding and absurdity in this work. Furthermore nothing in this work represents legal advice, it is solely a piece of research on a word which touches on topics in law.

Part 1

<u>What is this thing we call a "person"</u>

Introduction

The simplest way to begin this enquiry is to state the obvious. What is the obvious? Simply put, we use the word person to refer to a Human Being. If we look to any Standard English dictionary we see the primary definition of person, i.e. the first in the list of definitions, as a human being; nothing contentious in this. This is what the common man believes and is told, taught, shown and indoctrinated into believing, as a child, what a *person* is. Yet this is from where the confusion or obfuscations, whatever you want to call it, arises. From this perturbation a lot of misunderstanding and injustice is born. A quote from James Mitchell sums up the situation quite succinctly:

"And what is this person or persona of which we hear so much? Most people are now inclined to adopt the view of Max Müller. Nothing can be more abstract: it is neither male nor female, neither young nor old. As a noun it is hardly more than what to be is as a verb. In French it may even come to mean nobody ; for if we ask our concierge at Paris if anyone has called on us during our absence he will reply "Personne, monsieur!" which means "Not a soul, sir !"[1]

Etymology and History of the word "person"

So, now I think it is incumbent on us to look to the origins of the word before we begin to elaborate on the other various definitions of the word "person." To do this we will look in to the etymological history of the word and its evolution. Basically, etymology will give us an account of the conception of a word and its original use, as sometimes old words were just compounded to form a new word. This will become more apparent as we journey further back in time, and of course with word time travelling we must also take the epochs into account how the word was used.

First we must recognise that the words *person* and *persona* in today's usage are intimately related of a sort, for they arise from the same mother, and are brothers of a kind. It is documented that these words *person/persona* have their origin in Latin, which in turn is borrowed from the Greek equivalent.

---

[1] Significant Etymology by James Mitchell (1908), footnote, William Blackwood and Sons. P.237-239

Of course, all this began within the world of theatre in Greece where "religion was the cradle of Drama." [2] The Greek triad of their history, religion and culture was represented in the theatre with the actors representing the various roles. However to do this disguises were needed and so became an integral part of the relevant depictions were, and as Hastings (1901) says:

"...the most important part of the disguise was the mask, by means of which the actor's countenance could be distinguished at a distance, and which made it possible for the same person to play different parts by making repeated changes.' This device was particularly apt for men who had to play the part of women." [3]

Thus the mask was a vital feature needed for the representation of the appropriate character. But what importance does this have to our inquiry? Well it is the Greek word for mask that is important. The word used for mask was *prosopon*. This simply is translated as 'what is before the face', *pros* meaning before and *opon* meaning face.

Now as time passed the Romans slowly adopted the theatre into their own culture, translating many Greek works into Latin. Yet there were differences, for example, the Romans did not wear masks at the genesis of their theatre, but, after time the wearing of masks was adopted. That which was not adopted was the Greek word for mask. Instead the Romans named their mask 'persona', which is the combination of two words, the first being *'per'* meaning 'through or by means of'; and *'sono,'* which meant to sound. Thus the word *personare* literally meant through-sounders [4]. The reason behind this definition was that because these masks, both in Greece and Italy, used some apparatus which lay behind the mask, which helped channel and augment the volume of the actor's voice, which was entirely necessary in an open amphitheatre.

Thus the word persona was born. Later it was to become the mother to various children. Yet, as a noun, a persona was simply a physical mask made from thin wood or clay, made into various countenances, nothing more, and nothing less. If it had stayed that way then this work would not be necessary, nevertheless it has changed and evolved into more than what it used to be.

So now we have the origin of the word and with a little history to back it up, yet we must see why it came into use in England. For it was the roman occupation which, began in 55 B.C., that planted the seed for Latin to move into

[2] The theatre, its development in France and England, and a history of its Greek and Latin origins by Charles Hastings (1901) Duckworth & Co. P. 1

[3] Ibid,.16

[4] Significant Etymology by James Mitchell, 1908, footnote, William Blackwood and Sons. P.237-239

the language of Britain. However the Romans were not to stay forever in the land of Britain, but as H.M. Scarth has said in his work *Roman Britain*.

"The most enduring record of Roman times, and the change wrought by Roman conquest throughout the civilised world, is the adoption of the Roman letters of the alphabet, which have been used ever since." [5]

It was language that was the legacy of the Roman Empire, and as well as a few ruins and roads, but one significant part of the legacy lies in this simple word *person*. Naturally with the Norman Conquest and the introduction of French into England we have a reinforcement of another Latin based language adding to the richness and complexities of the English language itself, a language that was in the process of evolving. But as we see in our quote from James Mitchell above the word *personne* in French is translated as nobody into English.

Now we have two words in our language today *person* and *persona*. It is clear these two words are related and from where the relationship stems. Yet it is the word *persona* that hasn't strayed far from its original form, but it does give us a clue as to why *person* has changed so much. Persona as we define it today simply means a role or character we assume in certain situations. For example, a boss must adopt a persona when he works, which can be completely different from his personality at home. In such situations people adopt these personas to help them accomplish something, or protect themselves from something. A persona is something we put on and take off when necessary, as was the case with the masks in Ancient Greece and Rome.

So we can see a simple shift in the meaning of *persona*, originally as mask, to its current meaning of a role or character; a shift is so subtle most people in society are totally oblivious to it. This is also so shown by the phrase *dramatis personae* and *Persona non grata*, which are still used today. Is it not easy to see how this could happen? Yet when we turn to *person* we have a more difficult time of tracking its changes through the ages. It is now that we turn to the works of the etymologists to provide clarity. Etymology, as mentioned above, is simply the study of historical linguistic change, and from their hard work we can begin to look more into the history of the *person*.

First we must diverge somewhat from our theme and look into various themes of etymology that will provide us with some clarification. Greenough and Kittridge in their work *'Words and their ways in English speech'* [6] give us some

---

[5] *Roman Britain* by H.M. Scarth, p. 178

[6] Words and their ways in English speech by Greenough and Kittridge, (1902), Macmillan and Co.

clues on how words change in relation to their original meaning, yet keep their connection to the original source of meaning. One of the concepts they use is called radiation, which means at the core is the original meaning of the word and its subsequent words are off-shoots, like rays from the sun. They are all connected to the source yet they are not the source. A good example of this that Greenough and Kittridge give of this is the word *power*. The word originally comes from the Latin '*potere*', which means 'to be able', and of course in modern Italian the same word is still used. From this the old French word *pouer* (the modern French is *pouvoir*) *from which* our word power comes, probably from when Old French became an important language in the British Isles. One can look to other Latin based languages and see the similarities, for example in Spanish '*poder*' is the equivalent of the English 'to be able' or 'can' in its verb form but as a noun it means power. So for example the Spanish sentence "*poder tener el poder*" literally means 'to be able to have the power.' Now all derivations of the word power all come from the source meaning, which is to be able to do something or have the capacity to do something. This is how radiation of a word works.

The next clue Greenough and Kittridge give us to how *person* has changed is, in their words, thus

"the next process that we have to study, in which a word moves gradually away from its first meaning by successive steps of alternate specialization and generalization until, in many cases, there is not a shadow of connection between the sense that is finally developed and that which the term bore at the outset." [7]

To try and put this in the simplest of terms, we have a word with a meaning which we will call (A) which is modified by a slightly different usage, which we shall call (B). Thus,

"...a word may get a new meaning by the addition of a modifying idea (expressed or implied) to the old one." [8]

This is where can begin to see how *person* has changed, with a successive set of different usages. Greenough and Kittridge show how *person* started off by meaning a mask until it came to mean a *parson* (a member of the clergy), by using this method of successive steps of usage. They provide an enlightening method of showing the steps, which are laid out below.

---

[7] Words and their ways in English speech by Greenough and Kittridge, (1902), Macmillan and Co, p. 259

[8] Ibid, p. 265

1.	A	A mask
2.	A+B	character indicated by mask
3.	B	character or role in (play)
4.	B+C	one who represents a character
5.	C	a representative in general
6.	C+D	a representative of church in Parish
7.	D	Parson [9]

From this illustration we can see the source of *person* as a mask (A) and because of this usage in theatre, the character and the mask (A+B) joined themselves in meaning. We in modern English often use the word mask to mean that someone is concealing something, which is what the Greek actors did by assuming a character with the mask. This then evolved in to *person* meaning a character or role(C), in which the word *persona* we still retain this definition. However *person* morphs once again into the one who represents the character (B+C) until we are left with just a representative in general(C). Of course this meaning (C) can be used in many different ways as we will see later in this work. But to follow on with Greenough and Kittridge reasoning we now see *person* being used to mean a representative of church in a parish (C+D) which naturally leads to a person being called a parson. We can see this usage if we look into John Cowell's Law dictionary entitled '*The interpreter of words and terms*' (published in 1607) where if we look up the word person we see the words 'See Parson'. So it was not but some 400 years ago that in English *person* meant parson, not the human being as we know and recognise the word today.

Hopefully you are getting a clearer idea of the changing nature of the word *person* and its interesting evolution. Yet the most important aspect we can take from Greenough and Kittridge's work is that *person* at the core revolves around representing something. For the mask represents a specific character, a character represents a certain figure, be it real or mythical; a parson represents the church. This we can see by Greenough and Kittridge's theory of the radiation of a word.

Of course the story does not end here we have another somewhat 400 years of evolution of the *person* to explain away. We have seen the development from its original meaning of mask to come to mean parson, so:

"*...we no longer think of masks but of the real characters appearing in a play. After all, an actor wearing a mask of the king was for the time being a king, and thus persona came to mean the very opposite of mask viz., a man's real nature and character.*" [10]

[9] Words and their ways in English speech by Greenough and Kittridge, (1902), Macmillan and Co, p. 265
[10] Ibid p. 268

There were subtle shifts in meaning, like we saw above, where the fiction has become a reality, what was once unreal has now become real. Maybe this can be explained by the word character. This was originally taken from the Greek word *Kharakter* meaning an engraved mark, until the meaning was expanded by metaphor to mean a defining quality.[11] Thus a character became to mean a defining quality which was why it was used in theatre to signify the role an actor was playing, and of course the mask was definitely a defining quality. This is an important aspect when we think of somebody's character nowadays. For it could be a trait by which we recognize someone, or the sum of traits that define a man, which we tend to call a personality now (yet another intrusion of the pesky *person*). Now we can see that *personality* is a set of defining qualities that creates an identity. As we all know, *Ident* in Latin means *same*, and the *–ify suffix* comes from Latin verb to make, so it literally means 'to make the same.' So when we identify with something we make it the same! Sounds Strange I know, but look at what happens when a person asks for your identification, is it not to make sure you are the same man that you claim to be. To make the same, is the simplest definition and our identity is what we have created, what we have made to be us.

Can we not argue now then that when *person* was in usage as a parson his character or defining quality held some prestige? For was not the church at this time wielding immense power? The house or office of the parson was called a parsonage, which in turn is related to the word personage, which means someone with high status or rank. Someone with high status or rank was usually associated to some title or office they held, for example, a king or queen. Can we not extend, with some liberty on my part, on Greenough and Kittridge's diagram to aid us in tracing our flighty friend *person*?

1.	A	A mask
2.	A+B	character indicated by mask
3.	B	character or role in (play)
4.	B+C	one who represents a character
5.	C	a representative in general
6.	C+D	a representative of church in Parish
7.	D	a parson
8.	D+E	a parson with high rank or office
9.	E	someone with high rank or office
10.	E+F	high rank/office has status
11.	F	someone with status

---

[11] http://www.etymonline.com

For example, in Booth's *Analytical dictionary of the English language* he states that

"...the term personage is more applicable to one who is officially raised above the multitude. It is, therefore, more select and better fitted than "person" to denominate one of the higher orders of society. In the same sort of etiquette the plural, persons rises above the word PEOPLE: *the latter being always collective, while the former are separately considered in the mind. "Twenty people are a multitude; but the phrase "twenty persons' suggests the idea that each may possess a different character."* [12]

The meaning of the *person* is subtly shifting and as we are beginning to see the changes occurring before our eyes, we notice how the word aligns with its historical use. The Meaning shown in E and F are to be taken seriously now, not only for their meaning but for their historical use. For it should be known in English history by everyone who reads this work that one thing we English are known for is its repressive class system. During some turbulent historical times the class system has oppressed the mass of the population for the benefit of the upper classes. Those people who bore some form of status were *persons*, gentlemen, officials, and the aristocracy, for example. This, however, we will delve more into in the second part of this essay.

Although the word *person* has more usages in modern English we have for the moment traced its historical meaning and evolution enough to be able to explain its modern usage.

Modern usage of the word "person"

Now we must look to today and how *person* is utilized in modern English. As mentioned when we began to look at the history of the word, our modern and primary use of *person* is to mean a human being. That was what I was taught the word meant and I am sure most can concur with my own empirical observation regarding this. Below are some of the definitions of the word *person* taken from a dictionary easily accessible to everyone. [13]

---

[12] Analytical dictionary of the English language by David Booth, 1835, Cochrane and Co., p. cvi
[13] http://dictionary.reference.com/

per·son –noun

1. A human being, whether man, woman, or child: The table seats four persons.

2. A human being as distinguished from an animal or a thing.

3. *Sociology.* An individual human being, esp. With reference to his or her social relationships and behavioural patterns as conditioned by the culture.

4. *Philosophy.* A self-conscious or rational being.

5. The actual self or individual personality of a human being: You ought not to generalize, but to consider the person you are dealing with.

6. The body of a living human being, sometimes including the clothes being worn: He had no money on his person.

7. The body in its external aspect: an attractive person to look at.

8. A character, part, or role, as in a play or story.

9. An individual of distinction or importance.

10. A person not entitled to social recognition or respect.

11. *Law.* A human being (natural person) or a group of human beings, a corporation, a partnership, an estate, or other legal entity (artificial person or juristic person) recognized by law as having rights and duties.

12. *Grammar.* A category found in many languages that is used to distinguish between the speaker of an utterance and those to or about whom he or she is speaking. In English there are three persons in the pronouns, the first represented by I and we, the second by you, and the third by he, she, it, and they. Most verbs have distinct third person singular forms in the present tense, as writes; the verb be has, in addition, a first person singular form am.

13. *Theology.* Any of the three hypostases or modes of being in the Trinity, namely the Father, the Son, and the Holy Ghost.

We have **thirteen** definitions of the word *person* not one as generally perceived, because if you ask most people what a person is you find that they will give the first definition in our list. So how do we get from something meaning a mask to meaning a human person, well this will be explained in the second part of this work.

Let us look to our second usage which is 'a human being as distinguished from an animal or a thing.' We can suggest here that the notion of *person* is used in the sense of a defining quality, simply meaning not an animal or thing. The placing of the words human being is irrelevant in the meaning, for if you are not an animal or a thing (including nature under the class of things) then what are you?

Definitions 3 and 4 I will not discuss as they come under fields not entirely relevant to this work.

The fifth definition given 'The actual self or individual personality of a human being,' does not refer to the physical human being but to a something more transient, more ephemeral. Our personality is not a fixed quality it changes over time. Ask this question to yourself, "Am I the same as I was when I was a child, a teenager, a young adult, a middle aged adult, etc." What would your response be? I think most of us realize that we evolve and change our personality. The qualities that define you come and go, sometimes they stay and are repressed, and sometimes they evolve. The important point to take from this is the use of the word *personality*.

Definitions 6 and 7 can be looked at together as they are related. The sixth definition states that person can mean 'The body of a living human being, sometimes including the clothes being worn.' This is a strange way to define *person* but, if we look back to the previous section on the history and etymology of the word *person*, we can see how this may connect to the original few meanings. A body in religious terms is often seen as a mere vessel for the soul, self, atman, whatever you want to call it. As Shakespeare says:

"All the world's a stage, and all the men and women merely players. They have their exits and their entrances; and one man in his time plays many parts" [14]

---

[14] As You Like It by William Shakespeare, 1599, Act II, Scene VII

Many people in the past, and still do today, have viewed the body as a vessel, a thing that embodies the soul, like the actor embodies the character he plays, which again brings us to the notion of the *person* being a mask or character. As to the clothes, well these can be recognised as part of the mask or character. All this applies to the seventh definition of 'The body in its external aspect.'

The eighth definition 'A character, part, or role, as in a play or story,' should be self explanatory by now so I will not comment on this.

The ninth definition, 'An individual of distinction or importance,' we can see by looking at my extension of Greenough and Kittridge's diagram that *person* developed into someone of status, thus an individual of distinction and importance. You can now see how some of the definitions connect by subtle shifts in meaning or radiate from the original meaning.

Looking at the tenth definition we might be puzzled by as to why *person* can come to mean 'A person not entitled to social recognition or respect.' It would be my supposition that this comes from the phrase *persona non grata*, where it was first used by diplomats who were not welcome in the countries to which they were sent. Of course the phrase was then extended to a person of some group who were not welcomed by some action the performed and thus were stripped of any social recognition or respect. But again this is just a supposition on mt part

The eleventh definition we will be looking at in part II of this work so it is not expedient for us to review this definition here.

As for the last two definitions these have no bearing on the subject at hand, for this work does not seek to clarify grammar or theology.

So now we have looked at some standard definitions and to some extent have looked at them in parallel with the etymology of the word *person*. Hopefully we have a better understanding of the how the word began and its evolution.

The only other thing we must mention here is from the family of the *person*, which is another ubiquitous word and that is *personality*, which is mentioned above. Although we will not be looking into it more thoroughly as was done with the word *person*, it is something that is intimately related to the concept of a *person*. We can see that this noun comes from the adjective of *personal*, which simply put means pertaining to the *person*. Personality therefore is an expansion on the adjective form, which again, simply put is the characteristics which pertain to the *person*. Characteristic is used in the sense of defining qualities as we have mentioned above.

The story does not end there though as another insidious concept must be raised to explain modern usage; the issue of political correctness.

Political correctness, Language and the 'person'

Now it is not for me to judge the merits and pitfalls of political correctness, but since the phrase contains the word 'political' one must be dubious of its intent. It has been a trend in this movement of political correctness to turn the common words into terms we must avoid using so as not to cause offence. *Person* is one of these new terms of the political correctness movement. *Person* is used place of words such as man or woman, boy or girl and even Human Being, to avoid using such offensive language. Thus the word *person* is perfect for the advocates of political correctness, for as we quoted before:

"Nothing can be more abstract: it is neither male nor female, neither young nor old" [15]

But what is the concept of political correctness and where did it come from? There seems to be no single consensus on the definition of political correctness, but some say it stems from the Frankfurt school and cultural Marxism and has its birth around the era of the First World War,[16] whether this is true in is not for me to debate. But a definition by Atkinson is quite illustrative:

"Political Correctness (PC) ... was a spontaneous declaration that particular ideas, expressions and behaviour, which were then legal, should be forbidden by law, and people who transgressed should be punished...It started with a few voices but grew in popularity until it became unwritten and written law within the community. With those who were publicly declared as being not politically correct becoming the object of persecution by the mob, if not prosecution by the state." [17]

This insidious concept of political correctness is without doubt a political tool for as Orwell says:

"...the decline of a language must ultimately have political and economic causes" [18]

The decline of the English language can easily be recognised by the use of political correctness as a tool to control the way people think and therefore act. As

---

[15] Significant Etymology by James Mitchell, (1908), footnote, William Blackwood and Sons. P.237-239
[16] The Origins of Political Correctness An Accuracy in Academia Address by Bill Lind, 2000
[17] Political Correctness by Philip Atkinson, http://www.ourcivilisation.com/pc.htm
[18] George Orwell: 'Politics and the English Language' First published: *Horizon*. GB, London., April 1946

15

stated previously the use of the words man, women, boy, girl, female, male, etc, are "politically incorrect" because of what they call sexism. So to avoid that this wonderful little word *person* arrives to solve this problem. How convenient! Yet, unknown by many, the word *person* has severe implications in law as you will soon see in the next two parts of this work.

This introduction of politically correct words does not limit itself only to the word *person*. Another example is the use of the word individual, which technically is an adjective, but used as a noun it now refers to a *person*. Orwell describes this as pretentious diction and he states that:

"Words like *phenomenon, element, individual (as noun), objective, categorical, effective, virtual, basic, primary, promote, constitute, exhibit, exploit, utilize, eliminate, liquidate,* are used to dress up a simple statement and give an air of scientific impartiality to biased judgments."[19]

You will see much of this pretentious diction in the English language today, especially in the field of law. Orwell gives another astonish example of how language can be subverted:

"*Here is a well-known verse from Ecclesiastes:*

I returned and saw under the sun, that the race is not to the swift, nor the battle to the strong, neither yet bread to the wise, nor yet riches to men of understanding, nor yet favour to men of skill; but time and chance happeneth to them all.

Here it is in modern English:

Objective considerations of contemporary phenomena compel the conclusion that success or failure in competitive activities exhibits no tendency to be commensurate with innate capacity, but that a considerable element of the unpredictable must invariably be taken into account."[20]

Language is a potent force in human culture and the abuse of cannot be condoned, for the sake of not offending someone. For what might offend one man may pass over the head of the next. This can be highlighted by the eminent philosopher of language, Ludwig Wittgenstein, when he says

"*...the meaning of a word is its use in the language.*"[21]

[19] Ibid
[20] Ibid
[21] Philosophical Investigations by Ludwig Wittgenstein, 1953, Basil Blackwell Ltd, p. 20

This is an important concept and must be recognized in the context of this work. As you have seen when the modern definitions were elucidated, there are thirteen definitions, or better to say there are thirteen ways in which the word *person* is used modern English. So one can suggest that dictionaries do not define word or specify what a word is, rather it show its use in language. Now language is a subtle creature where confusion arises easily, this has been explained by the thinker Alfred Korzybski with his famous statement of which I am paraphrasing 'the map is not the territory and words are not the things they represent.' Or as Korzybski states himself:

"If words are not things, or maps are not the actual territory, then, obviously, the only possible link between the objective world and the linguistic world is found in structure, and structure alone. The only usefulness of a map or a language depends on the similarity of structure between the empirical world and the map-languages. If the structure is not similar, then the traveller or speaker is led astray, which, in serious human life-problems, must become always eminently harmful,. If the structures are similar, then the empirical world becomes 'rational' to a potentially rational being, which means no more than that verbal, or map-predicted characteristics, which follow up the linguistic or map structure, are applicable to the empirical world."[22]

What Korzybski is basically saying here is if some words do not conform to how we naturally use them then confusion will arise which in turn can affect the minds of people. I use a simple maxim taken from the works of Wittgenstein and Korzybski and apply it when necessary, which is:

"The word is not the thing it represents but gets its meaning from its use"

In regards to political correctness, it is obvious language is being used for a political agenda. Its use of the word *person* is obviously for some political gain, but this will be seen in the next sections of this work. But from the point of view of modern usage the word *person* is being used to outlaw such terms as Human being, man, woman, girl, boy, etc. By replacing these words with *person* it is trying to make is into abstract entities; one homogenous group.

Orwell predicted this control of language in his famous novel 1984, and it now can be seen in the form of political correctness. For we must not forget that language frames our thoughts which in turn influence our actions as Orwell clearly pointed out in his novel, which I recommend highly to anyone who has not already read it.

---

[22] Science and Sanity by Alfred Korzybski, 5th Edition, Institute of General semantics, 1994, p. 61

Language, when abused and manipulated, infects the whole of society and to isolate to certain fields, as that of law, and change the use of words can only be of detrimental effect on people and the society they live in.

Conclusion of Part 1

So to sum up this first part of our work the word *person* is an abstract word, as we have seen by its chameleon-like changes of the centuries. We have seen that we have this family of words; *person, persona, personal, personality, etc.* We have seen the birth of the concept of a *person* and its evolution throughout quite a few centuries. We have also seen the modern usages of the words as well as hwo political correctness has cemented this abstraction in the minds of many, by using the excuse of feminism, ageism or any –ism that applies. We now use the word *person* as a neutral term.

Yet it still hasn't answered our original question. Why do we call a human being a *person*? Don't worry as this will soon be addressed. This cannot be answered now because what has been written so far is just a piece of the puzzle. The following centuries leading up to now will begin to give us a clearer understanding. However we must veer away from the world of etymology and general language, and to do this we must undertake an examination of the word person as used in English law.

Part 2

Law and the "person"

Introduction

I think to begin this section, which is really the 'meat and bones' of the confusion of the use of the word *person*. I will leave it to Salmond who says it best in his work on jurisprudence.

"It is not permissible to adopt the simple device of saying that a person means a human being, for even in the popular or non-legal use of the term there are persons who are not men" [23]

This is where our confusion begins. Why is it not permissible to say that a person is a human being? For in the first section the primary usage of *person* is a Human Being yet now we are being told that it is too simple use it like this in law

To discover this conundrum we must delve into certain aspects of law. The law is a complicated area for any layperson to understand which is why an industry has arisen around it, and anyone not privy to the information this industry has will be lost in a labyrinth of language that will tie your mind up in knots. Many refer to this language as 'Legalese,' and see it as completely foreign. Personally I do not hold this view since language is a complex entity and cannot be pigeonholed so easily. So let us look first to the language of law to unravel the ball of knots it appears to be before we move onto the topic of the *person* and the law.

The Language of Law

First we must look at the language of the law as it is language that breathes life into the law. Language is used to write the law; to discuss the law; to arbitrate the law and finally to define the law. One cannot escape the fact that in these days law and language are inseparable.

As mentioned previously it is said that legalese resembles a foreign language. Why do people say this? Well because if one does not understand a language it is foreign to them, or a better way of saying it is that it is unfamiliar or strange to them. Legalese is better referred to as a technical language. Other technical languages can be found in such fields as medicine, science, mathematics, engineering, etc. However we do not refer to these languages in these specific

---

[23] Jurisprudence and the law by John Salmond, second edition, Steven and Hayes, 1907, p. 275

fields as foreign, just unfamiliar to the layman. It is this unfamiliarity that causes all the problems when approaching the area of law. We expect what we read to mean the same thing as we assume it means to everybody familiar with the English Language, yet this is not the case. Everyday usage of one word can mean something entirely different in the eyes of the law, and thus our problem begins. It is through this problem that we have these people we call lawyers, the ones trained in law, unfortunately a lot of these people are unaware of this technical language as well; so more problems arise.

Why do we talk of such things as legalese? Well simply because the *person* in law is a technical term and a highly controversial one at that. Of course it has been argued that because there are law dictionaries then Legalese must be a foreign language. But that is just not the case. I think many people think that because there is a dictionary then a separate language must be associated with it. A dictionary, as we commonly think of it, is merely a chronicle of a language, it tells us what a word means and its various usages, if it has them. Without language a dictionary would have no meaning. Yet this is just one type of dictionary, another is a translation dictionary where the word in one language is translated into a different language. Finally there are technical dictionaries, which define words used in the specific field it is used for; a law dictionary is one of these types.

We must not be fooled into believing that because we are ignorant of some parts of our language, (and by ignorant I mean 'not know something') we cannot say that it is a separate language altogether, this would be just too facile to assume. We must remember our maxim:

"The word is not the thing it represents but gets its meaning from its use"

If one is not involved in the field of law then the language and expressions will confuse the most intelligent man or woman. The use of specifically defined usage can be explained by the above maxim. If you do not use the technical language of law, it will appear foreign to you.

In this work we will view Legalese as a technical language, and will use the appropriate resources for reference to legal terms and not ordinary usage. For, as we have seen, the use of words in law can be far different from common usage. Whether this is done deliberately or by necessity, we do not know. However comparisons will be made between the technical terms and ordinary usage to indicate the disparity between the same words. A separate work is indeed needed on language and the law, but that is for the future.

The legal definition of 'person'

As you saw from Salmond's quote[24] not all persons are human beings and it is this division which causes many problems as you will see further on in this work. It is this enigma of the word *person* in law that initiated research into this part of our language. The legal definition is slightly different than would be the normal assumption.

As the ordinary meaning of *person*, explained in the first part, has many usages, in law we are met with two usages of the word. The legal definition is dual in nature, changed by adjectives. The first definition or usage is what is called a *'natural person'* and the second a *'legal person,'* so you see it is not as simple as might think. After all you can't define something by using the same word you're trying to define.

The *natural person* simply refers to a human being. By adding the adjective 'natural' it means a person who is of nature, and up until now that has only been human beings. Although there is a current debate going on in different places to give animals a legal personality; so would animals become a natural person? The adjective 'natural' is more of a narrowing down of the definition of *person* to specify mankind. This definition is plain and is probably why we refer to ourselves as persons, but we are a long way off from explaining why this is the case.

The *legal person,* sometimes called an *artificial person,* is a different matter altogether and it will be the major aim of this work to show why. Simply put a *legal person* is a corporation in modern parlance, or as the English calls it, a body corporate. Now as you can see this is a big leap from calling a human being a person to calling a corporation a person.

Another word which must be introduced is that of *individual,* once an adjective now a noun, used to refer to a single human being, but also in law it can mean a individual legal person. It entirely depends on the context.

Now you can see how the law divides the concept of the *person* into two distinct entities. However to adopt these definitions is too easy to explain what a *person* in law really is.[25] What we must do instead is forget the definitions the dictionaries give us and delve deeper into the more general science of law, which is called Jurisprudence.

---

[24] Jurisprudence and the law by John Salmond, second edition, Steven and Hayes, 1907, p. 275
[25] A list of Defintions will be given in Appendix A

Jurisprudence and the 'person'

As explained above Jurisprudence is the science of the law, or sometimes called the theory or philosophy of law. Its aim is to help explain what law is and its varied constituents. So in this section we will see, from the view of Jurisprudence, what a *person* really is under the eyes of the law.

First of all Salmond talks of the nature of legal personality[26] before he speaks of *persons*. Now if we remember from above on the subject of personality it was said that personality was "the characteristics which pertain to the *person*." So when we talk of legal personality we can assume this to mean the legal characteristics that pertain to the *person*. It is then natural to find out what these legal characteristics are in order to elaborate on why a *person* has these characteristics attached to them.

Pollock states that,

"Law necessarily deals with duties and rights of persons"[27]

or as Salmond says:

"So far as legal theory is concerned, a person is any being whom the law regards as capable of rights and duties"[28]

As two of the leading authors on Jurisprudence have said it seems that duties and rights may be some of these defining qualities that might lead us to find out the nature of what a legal personality is.

So we have first to uncover what are *rights* and what are *duties* before we can proceed to attach these to our controversial *person*.

Rights, Duties and the 'person'

It must be said first that in law rights and duties go hand in hand, they are not two separate things that can be divided and investigated without referring to each other. So when we speak of a right there is a duty involved. But it must be

---

[26] Jurisprudence and the law by John Salmond, second edition, Steven and Hayes, 1907, p. 275
[27] A first book of Jurisprudence, by Sir Frederick Pollock, second edition, 1904, Macmillian and Co. p. 108
[28] Jurisprudence and the law by John Salmond, second edition, Steven and Hayes, 1907, p. 275

also noted that rights always have duties ascribed to them, duties on the other hand do not always have rights attached to them. [29]

Before going more in depth in the area of rights and duties there is another concept that must be considered first, and that is of wrongs. A wrong is as it suggests, a wrong act; it is the same in law as in ordinary life; it's just the details that differ, or as Salmond puts it:

"A wrong is simply a wrong act - an act contrary to the rule of right and justice. A synonym of it is injury, in its true and primary sense of injuria (that which is contrary to jus), though by a modern perversion of meaning this term has acquired the secondary sense of harm or damage (damnum) whether rightful or wrongful, and whether inflicted by human agency or not."[30]

These wrongs as they are known are of two types, moral and legal. A moral wrong would be, for example, murder because it is immoral to kill another human being by natural law theory. This is shown in our own system of common law. A Legal wrong on the other hand does not conform to natural law and comes solely from the minds of men. As Salmond says:

"A legal wrong is an act which is legally wrong, being contrary to the rule of legal justice and a violation of the law. It is an act which is authoritatively determined to be wrong by a rule of law, and is therefore treated as a wrong in and for the purposes of the administration of justice by the state"[31]

Maybe a good example of a legal wrong would be speeding tickets as it is a controversial topic in England nowadays. There is nothing morally wrong with speeding, unless it endangers lives; for there are some animals on earth which can break the speed limits but I doubt they will be fined. There are many legal wrongs which are not morally wrong, but the more laws a country has the more wrongs it creates. A wrong is such that if anyone should commit a wrong a punishment will be meted out by the state.

So here we have defined what a wrong is, but what connection does this have to rights and duties? Well, a wrong was elucidated because a duty is simply another way of saying "don't do wrong," so when you do something wrong, whether morally or legally, you have failed to fulfill a duty. As wrongs are divided into moral and legal, so too are duties. You have a moral duty, which is not to do a moral wrong, and a legal duty, which is not to do a legal wrong. Of course this is a simplified explanation for the layman to understand but essentially that is what is meant when we talk of duties.

---

[29] Elements of Law by William Markby, sixth edition, Oxford press, 1905. p. 92
[30] Jurisprudence and the law by John Salmond, second edition, Steven and Hayes, 1907, p. 180
[31] Ibid, p. 180

Now we must turn to rights which are slightly more complicated in nature. But Pollock gives a glimpse of what a right is:

"Right is the correlative of duty. As duty is a burden imposed by law, so right is freedom allowed or power conferred by law."[32]

Or as Thomas in his book, *'A treatise on Universal Jurisprudence'* states:

"A right is that quality in a person which renders it just for him to possess certain things, or to do certain things, consistently with the laws"[33]

Rights following along with duties and wrongs are also divided into moral rights and legal rights. A breach of a moral right would result in a moral wrong, and a breach of a legal right would be a legal wrong. This shows us how rights and duties are connected, and the fact that a right involves some form of freedom, yet with conditions attached (the duty).

All these rights, wrongs and duties are divided up into moral and legal categories which make it even more confusing for the ordinary man who knows nothing of law. Understanding what has just been written is not an easy task, and what has been presented to you is in a highly condensed form to make it intelligible to the layman.

So why are rights and duties the defining qualities that make up the legal personality that Salmond attributes to a *person?* Well I think Salmond says it best of all:

"All that is right or wrong, just or unjust, is so by reason of its effects upon the interests of mankind, that is to say upon the various elements of human well-being, such as life, liberty, health, reputation, and the uses of material objects. If any act is right or just, it is so because and in so far as it promotes some form of human interest. If any act is wrong or unjust, it is because the interests of men are prejudicially affected by it. Conduct which has no influence upon the interests of any one has no significance either in law or morals."[34]

There we have it! As Pollock stated the law only deals with the rights and duties of *persons,* and as Salmond said only a being that is capable of rights and duties is a *person.*

It is now important to analyse this definition that the scholars of Jurisprudence have given us. We will use Salmond's definition as a starting point for our analysis. The first term he gives us is 'a being', and of course when we hear that we think of something that exists, which does not necessarily mean a human being, as a human being is but one type of being. Another way to

---

[32] A first book of Jurisprudence, by Sir Frederick Pollock, second edition, 1904, Macmillian and Co. p. 61

[33] A Treatisse of Universal Jurisprudence by John Penford Thomas, second edition, 1829, p. 21

[34] Jurisprudence and the law by John Salmond, second edition, Steven and Hayes, 1907, p. 72

describe a being is by the word entity, which is more of a neutral term, for it can apply to corporeal and incorporeal things at the same time. Thus we can see how there is a division between natural persons and legal persons as both can be called entities but not beings.

The next part of the definition is 'capable of', which if we look in any dictionary means "*having the ability or capacity for.*"[35] Now having the ability or capacity for something implies the choice to use the aforementioned. For having something and using it are two different things. For example, everyone has the ability or capacity for violence but it is their choice to use it or not.

So to try and give a more accurate definition to what a *legal personality* is and its defining qualities, in regards to the in law, would be to say that it is 'an entity with the ability or capacity to have rights and duties.'[36] So according to the theory of jurisprudence something or somebody must have these defining qualities to be defined as a *person* in law.

So now we must turn to what the law defines as *persons*, namely the *natural person* and the *legal person* and see if we can match them up to our definition of legal personality. We will also look into these concepts with more depth to gain a better understanding of what they are. For to truly understand these concepts and how they apply to the common man will benefit greatly to finding out if a *person* really is a human being.

Natural persons vs. Legal persons

Let's begin with *natural persons* as this is the least complex of the two to analyse. As mentioned above a *natural person* is said to be a human being, but can we really say this? When we use the adjective 'natural' we are adding more information to the preceding noun; the noun being *person*. If we look to any dictionary (I use the one provided by the internet because most people will have access to this) then we see that natural as an adjective means 'existing in or formed by nature.'[37] So if we use our definition of legal personality and combine it with the meaning of natural we have:

'An *entity existing in or formed by nature with the ability or capacity to have rights and duties*'

---

[35] http://dictionary.reference.com/browse/capable
[36] This is the defintion that will be used to describe a legal personality in law from now on
[37] http://dictionary.reference.com/browse/natural - primary definition used out of the 30 or so definitions

This can be said to be the true meaning of *natural person*. Now as you can see a human being is not mentioned in the definition, but can be implied from it as we exist in or have been formed by nature. Yet are we the only things formed by nature on the planet? No, of course not, but if you remember our last quote by Salmond, rights and duties are created by human interests and it is only the law that recognises human interests. Under the definition above everything in nature should be a *natural person*, but this is not the case. Yet there are some interesting cases when we turn to the issue of animals, pets or work animals, for example. When we have a pet, for illustration a dog, do they not have rights and duties ascribed to them? For we give the dog a right to security i.e. we protect its well being by housing and feeding it and its duty is not to harm us in return and to give us company. In this scenario we are the sovereign and the dog is the person, so we ascribe rights and duties to the person. And in a nutshell this is how things work in Britain now.

So what we can say about the *natural person* is that it may include human beings is but not limited to them by definition. For if we are to take our meaning of *natural person* to be consistent with what the law says, it would indicate that we, human beings, are but one group under a vast class of things.

Now we turn to the *legal person*, a more thorny issue at best. As mentioned earlier, the modern conception of a legal person is a corporation. Again this is just too simple of a device to adopt when talking of *legal persons*. Let us first adopt our definition of legal personality and apply it to the *legal person*. First of all we must find a definition of legal used as an adjective, turning to the dictionary used throughout this work we see that legal means 'permitted by law.'[38] Therefore we can assume a *legal person* to be;

'An entity permitted by law with the ability or capacity to have rights and duties'

This would seem to be a more accurate definition of what a *legal person* is. Yet by its definition its vagueness is apparent. What is an entity permitted by law? This usually means a corporation, which is too vague of a device to contemplate, so yet again it is incumbent on us to look into the nature of what a corporation is.

Corporations as Legal Persons

Corporations are known as either *legal persons* or *artificial persons*. Here we must turn to Blackstone's commentaries on the laws of England to have a better idea of what a corporation is. But first it is prudent to point that although

---

[38] http://dictionary.reference.com/browse/legal

companies can be corporations, not all corporations are companies, so please keep this in mind as we elucidate the concept of a corporation. Firstly as Blackstone says:

"The first division of corporations is into aggregate and sole. Corporations aggregate consist of many persons united together into one society, and are kept up by a perpetual succession of members, so as to continue forever...Corporations sole consist of one person only and his successors, in some particular station, who are incorporated by law, in order to give them some legal capacities and advantages, particularly that of perpetuity, which in their natural persons they could not have had."[39]

So we have two divisions of what a corporation is; aggregate and sole. Corporations aggregate are what we are more familiar with and is probably why we call a company or business a corporation, but as we shall see this is more of a modern phenomenon. The concept of a body corporate, as this is how a corporation aggregate is more commonly known in Britain, is a much older phenomenon. As with our contentious word *person* we can attribute the idea of a body corporate to the Romans. Its first uses came in the form of universities and colleges as Blackstone expounds.

"They were called universitates, *as forming one whole out of many individuals; or* collegia, *from being gathered together"*[40]

After this the church also adopted this form of organization, which still goes on today. For example, public corporations are what we refer to as municipal government, which tend to be towns, cities and boroughs, or as Arnold says

"A municipal corporation, therefore, is a civil corporation aggregate, established for the purpose of investing the inhabitants of a particular borough or place with the power of self-government and with certain other privileges and franchises."[41]

A corporation sole on the other hand,

".... consist of one person only and his successors, in some particular station, who are incorporated by law, in order to give them some legal capacities and advantages, particularly that of perpetuity, which in their natural persons they could not have had."[42]

---

[39] Commentaries on the Laws of England in Four Books by William Blackstone, Philadelphia: J.B. Lippincott Co., 1893, p. 467
[40] Ibid, p. 468
[41] A Treatise on the law relating to Municipal Corporations in England and Wales by Thomas Arnold, Third edition 1863, p. 3
[42] Commentaries on the Laws of England in Four Books by William Blackstone, Philadelphia: J.B. Lippincott Co., 1893, p. 469

The best example of this would be our very own Queen, or the Crown as the corporation is known as. In fact the queen comprises of several corporations sole. Some officials also have same status of corporation sole, such as secretaries of state and other government officials. I would go as far as to say the prime minister could have similar status but that cannot be proven at this time.

This idea of corporation sole is not widely known and as Salmond says:

"The chief difficulty in apprehending the true nature of a corporation of this description is that it bears the same name as the natural person who is its sole member for the time being, and who represents it and acts for it... Nevertheless under each of these names two persons live. One is a human being, administering for the time being the duties and affairs of the office. He alone is visible to the eyes of laymen. The other is a mythical being whom only lawyers know of, and whom only the eye of the law can perceive."[43]

So here we have two variations of corporations both endowed with legal status and are thus called *Legal Persons*, however they do have some dissimilarities to the *natural person*. One of these is immortality, for *natural persons* die, but *legal persons* do not. This was instigated to facilitate longevity of the corporate entity, otherwise the death of the individual members of a group, would mean the death of the corporation.

Unfortunately the field of corporations is too wide to go into any depth here but what has been said should clarify the issue somewhat. What it does show is that a *legal person* is, as our previous definition says, an entity permitted by law with the ability or capacity to have rights and duties. Now these *legal persons* generally have the same rights as *natural persons* with a few added perks.

So far we have defined what a *person* is under the eyes of the law and the duality of its nature into natural and legal. We now know that rights and duties are fundamental part of what makes up a legal personality and subsequently a *person*. So would it not be pursuant of us to find out what our rights are.

The Rights of a 'Person'

This subject is too deep for a perfect analysis of the rights of a *person*. But we will look at what some commentators on law have to say about the subject. Also you will find the human rights acts laid down by law in appendix B.

Blackstone in his commentaries divides the absolute rights of an individual i.e. In this case a *natural person* into three principal categories which are

---

[43] Jurisprudence and the law by John Salmond, second edition, Steven and Hayes, 1907, p.288

1. The right of personal security
2. The right of personal liberty
3. The right of private property

The first right as Blackstone says is:

"The right of personal security consists in a person's legal and uninterrupted enjoyment of his life, his limbs, his body, his health, and his reputation."[44]

As to the second right of:

"Personal security, the law of England regards, asserts, and preserves the personal liberty of individuals. This personal liberty consists in the power of locomotion, of changing situation, or moving one's person to whatsoever place one's own inclination may direct, without imprisonment or restraint, unless by due course of law."[45]

The final right according to Blackstone is

"The third absolute right, inherent in every Englishman, is that of property: which consists in the free use, enjoyment, and disposal of all his acquisitions, without any control or diminution, save only by the laws of the land."[46]

Now of course this was written in 1753, but they do cover what our basic rights are and most other rights elucidated in appendix B will fall under these three categories. Of course this is just a cursory glance at what Blackstone writes to be more thorough I suggest the reader to read his commentaries which can be easily found in the public domain.

Another author we have used extensively here also has some definitions of what our rights are. Salmond's list is as follows.[47]

1. Rights over material things
2. Rights in respect of one's own person
3. The right of reputation
4. Rights in respect of domestic relations
5. Rights in the respect of other's rights
6. Rights over immaterial property
7. Rights to services.

---

[44] Commentaries on the Laws of England in Four Books by William Blackstone, Philadelphia: J.B. Lippincott Co., 1893, p. 128
[45] Ibid p. 134
[46] Ibid, p. 139
[47] Jurisprudence and the law by John Salmond, second edition, Steven and Hayes, 1907, p.188-190

These are what Salmond suggests our rights are, whether this is true or not it is not my place to argue that. Only to elucidate what some authors have to state on the subject. As with Blackstone, Salmond's book can be found in the public domain if you want to have a deeper understanding.

So these are our rights, and our duties are not to commit wrongs in accordance with these rights. All this is what we say a *person* has in the eyes of the law. Now we must move on to how the *person* has evolved in the eyes of the law so we can connect with the first part of this work and the original question; is a human being a *person*?

A 'person' in the history of law

Remember the first quote in this part of the work by Salmond[48] where we cannot say that a *person* means a human being, hopefully the work up until now has shown part of why this is true. This section will deal more with how this specifically applies to man. But let's begin by a curious quote from Salmond:

> "...in the law this want of coincidence between the class of persons and that of human beings is still more marked. In the law there may be men who are not persons; slaves, for example, are destitute of legal personality, in any system which regards them as incapable of either rights or liabilities."[49]

So in the past it has been a fact that certain human beings were not considered *persons* under the eyes of the law. So by logical deduction anyone seen not possessing rights or liabilities was not a *person*. A liability here just means someone whom is responsible for committing a wrong i.e. he is liable (legally responsible) for that act of wrong.

Slaves as being the prime example of human beings not considered *persons*. Slavery has a long history and is too complicated to go into here. But considering when slavery was legally abolished it is not so long ago compared to the length of human history. I say legally abolished because although slavery is against the law of all nations that does not mean that the practice has stopped, especially in

---

[48] "It is not permissible to adopt the simple device of saying that a person means a human being, for even in the popular or non-legal use of the term there are persons who are not men". Jurisprudence and the law by John Salmond, second edition, Steven and Hayes, 1907, p. 275

[49] Jurisprudence and the law by John Salmond, second edition, Steven and Hayes, 1907, p. 275

developing countries. In England there has been a long history of slavery dressed up in a variety of names. For example:

"English people was divided after the Conquest[50] into two classes, the free and the serf."[51]

The serf was owned by his lord and was basically a slave, of course this practice of serfdom eventually faded by the aid of the church and the common law of the land (by custom). It also helped that these serfs were countrymen and therefore were afforded the rights that an Englishman held. However the next form of slavery was one of race. After the British Empire conquered a lot of the world many of those who were conquered became legal slaves. This was then taken over to America until the time of Abraham Lincoln and the emancipation of the slaves. Yet even though they were emancipated a lot of their rights were withheld which led to the civil rights movement in America.

Another group of human beings have also had their rights restricted at various times in History and they comprise of half the population at any given time; namely women. For a long time women were denied many of the rights of men. As was the case with the early catholic church under canon law, as Hecker states:

"The canon law reaffirms woman's subjection to man in no uncertain terms. The wife must be submissive and obedient to her husband. She must never, under penalty, of excommunication, cut off her hair, because "God has given it to her as a veil and as a sign of her subjection." A woman who assumed men's garments was accursed; it will be remembered that the breaking of this law was one of the charges which brought Joan of Arc to the stake."[52]

And as Hecker states in 1914

"The attitude of the Roman Catholic Church towards women's rights at the present day is practically the same as it has been for eighteen centuries. It still insists on the subjection of the woman to the man, and it is bitterly hostile to woman suffrage"[53]

Of course, times have changed and the rights of women have improved dramatically. For example it was less than 100 years ago that women fought for and won the right of suffrage (the right to vote). The subjugation of women has always and still is a contentious issue. Like so many topics, we have touched on

---

[50] Being the Norman conquest of 1066
[51] The British citizen: His rights and priviliges, a short history, 1885, E. & J.B. Young, p. 69
[52] A short history of women's rights, By Eugene Hecker, Second edition, 1914, G.P. Putman's sons, p. 106
[53] Ibid p. 117

only the surface of such immense issues, but they are used to illustrate that a *person* is not what it purports to be.

Today women are considered to be *natural persons* under the eyes of law with the equivalent rights that men hold. But this has been through a process of evolution like the word *person* itself.

Throughout history there has been through some form of suppression of a man or woman's rights, and this is no less true today. Yet it is unclear if the suppression of some rights strips the man of his legal personality altogether, if so then he would no longer be a *person* in the eyes of the law; but this is merely a supposition on my part.

Is a Person a Human Being in Law?

It is now we must begin to answer the question that was the impetuous for this work. We have seen the history and etymology of the word *person*, so we now know where it comes from and what it was used to up to a certain point. The point that left us was that a *person* was meant as someone with status like an official or personage. We then looked at the modern usages of the word, of which there are many. A lot of the meanings could be explained by the referring to the etymology of the word, others had no relevance to the present inquiry. But nothing explained why a *person* is a human being.

After this we had to look into law to find the next piece of the puzzle. What was discovered was not so simple. For there are *persons* who are not human beings, and there have been human beings who were not regarded as *persons*.

A more specific meaning of the word *person* was given by looking into the area of Jurisprudence, which we will restate here.

Person – *An entity with the ability or capacity to have rights and duties*

Law however has seen it necessary to divide this definition by either saying the entity is formed by nature or permitted by law, so we are left with the division of *natural person* and *legal persons*. Yet human being is still not apparent by this definition, and as was shown for thousands of years there have been an ineffable amount people who had no rights, therefore these slaves in the eyes of law, were not considered *persons*. It was only people of status that were considered *persons*. Thus we have the connection between where we left our etymological study how it has been relevant to look into the law. Now since only people of status were *persons* with the according rights and duties, those, by deduction, who had no rights, were not considered *persons*. It is only in the last 150 years or so that, at least in the western world, that all people have slowly gained all the rights a human being should have. This naturally makes them *persons* in the eyes of the law, which is why we can suppose that *person* (natural at least) means a human being. Yet this is technically not true if we follow the logic of language rather than the twisted logic of the law.

Let me try and explain. The first thing that should strike the reader is that noun *person* is used in a specific way. If we can compare it to another word this might clarify things, for example the word mammal. Now a human being is a mammal, but not all mammals are human beings. Do you see the difference? A mammal describes a class of things and not the things themselves; it is a type of category like furniture, liquids, plants, etc. A person is a class of things, or a category, nothing more. Now if we describe ourselves as a person, you only describe yourself as a member of a class of things. You could just as well say you are a mammal; a biped; an organism. If we take the example of the class of furniture then we can point to a chair and say it's a chair which is the most specific noun to describe it, but it is also furniture.

The problem is that we use the word *person* like we use the word chair; you see a man and women before you and you call him or her a person, a gender neutral term, and the word sticks. Another example to illustrate the point is that of water. Now water is a liquid, but when frozen it is a solid, when it boils it becomes gaseous. In different states it falls under different categories. This is similar to the *person*, when it is natural, something formed by nature; when legal, something permitted by law.

So basically comes down to this. A human being has the capacity to be a *person* if it fulfils the criteria i.e. having the ability or capacity for rights and duties, but it is not a human being per se. Just as an animal can be a mammal if it fulfils the criteria of being,

"*any vertebrate of the class Mammalia, having the body more or less covered with hair, nourishing the young with milk from the mammary glands, and, with the exception of the egg-laying monotremes, giving birth to live young.*"[54]

But not all animals are mammals. Again we must refer to our maxim, "*The word is not the thing it represents but gets its meaning from its use,*" thus we see that the word *person* is used differently in law than in ordinary modern usage. It's just that it seems not many involved in the field either know this or are willing to tell everyone this.

---

[54] http://dictionary.reference.com/browse/mammal

So in the eyes of the law a *person* is not a human being, it never has been and doubtfully will ever be. It is simply a class of things; nothing more nothing less. If we really want to be pedantic, *person* really holds its original use, a mask. For rights and duties, supposedly are given to us by our sovereign power, be it God, Allah, the state or yourself. You put on these rights, like a mask, which shows other people what you are, to be able to move around in a world full of other people wearing similar masks. To highlight this development we can use Greenough and Kittredges's diagram and extend it more.

1.	A	A mask
2.	A+B	character indicated by mask
3.	B	character or role in (play)
4.	B+C	one who represents a character
5.	C	a representative in general
6.	C+D	a representative of church in Parish
7.	D	a parson
8.	D+E	a parson with high rank or office
9.	E	someone with high rank or office
10.	E+F	high rank/office has status
11.	F	someone with status
12.	F+G	s/one with status has rights
13.	G	anyone with rights
14.	G+H	any entity with rights

To sum up this section, we have found a main part of the puzzle, debatable or not, that gives at least some clarity to the matter. In the third and final part of this work we will see how this applies to the common man by looking into some laws of England, seeing how they are interpreted and how this all applies to the *person*.

The next section will be the more demanding because we must delve more into the language of the law, which always produces a headache. This, nevertheless, is necessary to see how this one little word affects your life so profoundly.

Part 3

The Laws of Britain

Introduction

To put this section into context we will first begin by giving a small introduction to what the actual law of England is. From this basic understanding of how the law works will be of great utility, for the following sections is where we will go deeper into actual laws, how they are interpreted and what relevance this has to the *person*. This part will be the most technical of the three because we have to begin to introduce legal terms and explain their usage, so patience is required from the reader.

The two divisions of English law

It is said there are two divisions of law in England. The first being the more ancient system we know as Common Law and the second being the more modern Statute Law. So it is to these two divisions a cursory overview must be given, which we will start with the older of the two divisions: Common Law.

Common Law

Common law is generally known as the unwritten law of England (*Lex non-scripta*) for as Ruegg says:

"It originally consisted of a collection of unwritten maxims and customs, which were supposed to have existed immemorially in this country."[55]

So Common law is generally known as customary law as it derives its authority from the customs of the nation over time, which was never formally written down, like an act of parliament. A good example of this would be murder, for there is no written rule that murder is forbidden, but as a custom, and this being part of common law, it is forbidden to murder anyone. Blackstone divides these customs into three types

---

[55] An Elementary Commentary on English Law by Alfred Ruegg, 1920, George Allen & Unwin Ltd, p. 12

"This unwritten, or common, law is properly distinguishable into three kinds: 1.General customs; which are the universal rule of the whole kingdom, and form the common law, in its stricter and more usual signification. 2. Particular customs; which, for the most part, affect only the inhabitants of particular districts. 3. Certain particular laws; which, by custom, are adopted and used by some particular courts, of pretty general and extensive jurisdiction."[56]

These customs or laws were determined by judges, which why the common law is often referred to as Judge made law, or case law where precedents are set down as a guide for future generations to follow, as Ruegg says.

"Whether a custom, general or particular, is a part of the Common law of England, can only be finally declared by the judges, whose decisions when pronounced are afterwards binding upon themselves and all inferior courts."[57]

Of course this is not to say that everything is not written, but they do not include acts of parliament, for as Hale says:

"...when I call those parts of our laws leges non scripta, I do not mean as if those laws were only oral, or communicated from the former ages to the later, merely by word; for all those laws have their several monuments in writing, whereby they are transferred from one age to another, and without which they would soon lose all kind of certainty... But I therefore stile those parts of the law leges non scripta, because their authoritative and original institutions are not set down in writing in that manner or with that authority that acts of parliament are."[58]

So Common Law is the oldest system of law of England and continues today. Yet how does this connect to the other division of law we have today? Well to see this then we must look into the birth of the Parliament as they are the brach which write, enact and enforce statutes. Blackstone writes about the beginning of parliament,

"I hold it sufficient that it is generally agreed, that in the main the constitution of parliament, as it now stands, was marked out so long ago as the seventeenth year of king John, ad 1215, in the great charter granted by that prince"[59]

That isn't to say that before this time nothing of the like existed, but with the writing of the *Magna Charta* a general summons was issued to various personages by the king. Thus parliament was born and over it long history, which is of such a great volume to go deeply into here, we arrive at the state where we are today. Common

---

[56] Commentaries on the Laws of England in Four Books by William Blackstone, Philadelphia: J.B. Lippincott Co., 1893, p. 67

[57] An Elementary Commentary on English Law by Alfred Ruegg, 1920, George Allen & Unwin Ltd, p. 15

[58] The history of the common law of england by Matthew Hale, 1820, sixth edition, Butterworths, p. 21

[59] Commentaries on the Laws of England in Four Books by William Blackstone, Philadelphia: J.B. Lippincott Co., 1893, p. 149

Law is a complex entity and cannot be summed up lightly, it advisable to read up on the subject, where there are plenty of authoritative works in the public domain.

What we can say is that it is from common law that our next division of law derives its authority, namely Statute law.

Statute Law

Statute law is referred to as the written law (*Lex Scripta).* Since Ruegg puts it best we will let him give a concise explanation.

"*Statute law - Since Parliamentary government was fully established Statute law means the Acts of Parliament passed by the House of Lords and House of Commons, and assented to by the King. These Statutes have always necessarily been in writing or print, and thus collectively are called the Lex Scripta.*"[60]

So basically Statutes are acts of parliaments, of which there have been thousands of in its long history, although many have been repealed, or revised. However a statute is not simply an act of parliament. It is known that universities use statutes as the rules of their organisation, so it is not the sole domain of Parliament to have statutes.

The first written document to pass laws was the Magna Charta of 1215, this is debatable whether it is a statute, but it was the first form of written law. Subsequently a different version of the Magna Charta was put on the statute rolls, but not the original, which is one of the founding documents of the unwritten English Constitution.

Nowadays it would seem to the common man that Statute Law is the law of the land but one must make a distinction here between **the law** and **a law.** The law is what we think of as common law, whilst an act of parliament is a law, usually given the force of law. Statute Law was introduced to provide a remedy for a mischief that common law did not provide.

To make this is easier to understand an analogy might clarify things. Imagine a mighty oak tree. Now the roots are the customs and traditions of England that have developed over time. The trunk of the tree is the common law, which has grown bigger and bigger as the roots (customs) grow stronger. Now the branches and leaves can be compared to Statute Law. Simple enough, I hope! Now statutes come and go as no parliament can be bound by the previous one, like the branches and leaves

---

[60] Ibid, p. 11

which wither away and die when new shoots take over. The problem today is that people take the branches and leaves to be the whole of the tree, ignoring the trunk and the roots.

Statutes are the rules of society, which can be changed, and it is the law which enforces, or not, these rules. Never mistake the rules for the entity which enforces them. An example of this is that there is no statute for murder, for it has been an immemorial custom that murder is wrong, therefore it is under Common law. However, the "crime" of speeding is a statute law, enforced by common law, for driving fast is a new phenomenon, which common law had no remedy for.

The problem with statute law is that it is open to abuse by corrupt people for power, for if one can push through a law that is unjust, common law has to enforce it. This is what we are seeing happening today as thousands of new offences have been created since the seventies, to the point that every boy or child born in Britain will be a criminal at some point in their lives, unwillingly or not.

It was initially this imbalance of statute law that prompted this enquiry into the *person*.

This is a very simplistic overview of the two divisions of the English system of Law and it would benefit the reader to delve deeper into the subject for a better understanding, unfortunately this is beyond the scope of this work. What you do have is a simple understanding of how the system works, which was necessary for the proceeding part. For now we delve more into the world of statutes and see why it is relevant to the *person* and to the reader.

Statutory Definition of the "Person"

If one has ever read a statute, then you will know that when you do so you enter a labyrinth of language, consisting of twists, turns and dead ends. The language used by the draftsmen of such documents is a science in itself, as is the reading of them an art form. For this we have solicitors, barristers, lawyers, judges all to help us (please note the irony in this). But why cannot the common man simply read the law and be able to understand it? Simply because an industry would collapse, an industry that makes a lot of money every year.

So what does the word *person* have to do with statutes? The answer is everything. For statutes only deal with *persons*, the type we mentioned in the second part of this work; either the *natural person* or the *legal person*. All the things the law deals with lies under these two entities, so when one reads a statute a *person* will inevitably be mentioned or implied. This is the reason that understanding what the word *person* means is essential to the reader, because as will be shown a lot of vagueness arises in these acts of parliament which control our lives.

How then does a statute define what a person is? To do this the government has given us a hand in the form of the Interpretation act of 1978, this as the preamble (or synopsis) of the act:

"An Act to consolidate the Interpretation Act 1889 and certain other enactments relating to the construction and operation of Acts of Parliament and other instruments, with amendments to give effect to recommendations of the Law Commission and the Scottish Law Commission."[61]

Basically it helps out by giving some instructions to how acts of parliament are constructed. This is relevant to us because it also provides definitions of words used often, *person* being one of them. So let us delve further into this act and the construction and interpretation of statutes.

The Interpretation Act 1978

This 1978 act was a revision of the 1889 Interpretation act. It lays some clear guidelines on the construction of statutes, and consolidates certain ubiquitous terms. This was to aid the legislature in the drafting of future acts. An example of this is this provision.

"Any Act may be amended or repealed in the Session of Parliament in which it is passed."[62]

Or,

"In any Act, unless the contrary intention appears, —

(a) Words importing the masculine gender include the feminine;
(b) Words importing the feminine gender include the masculine;
(c) Words in the singular include the plural and words in the plural include the singular."[63]

---

[61] Interpretation Act 1978 (c.30), preamble
[62] Ibid, Section 2

The most important section to us is the following:

"In any Act, unless the contrary intention appears, words and expressions listed in Schedule 1 to this Act are to be construed according to that Schedule."[64]

To see the entirety of the act of this act look to Appendix C, but the relevant definition for us is hidden away in that schedule 1. The relevancy is that it defines the word *person* and how it should be interpreted, it is as follows:

"Person" includes a body of persons corporate or unincorporate.[65]

A small definition and concise definition, if we can even call it a definition, for it defines itself using the word *person* in the definition. So can we even call this is a definition? It looks more like guidance on how to use the word, not what it means. We will compare this with the original "definition" of the 1889 act, which is as follows:

"In this Act and in every Act passed after the commencement of this Act the expression "person" shall, unless the contrary intention appears, include any body of persons corporate or unincorporate"[66]

So we see that the original 1889 definition was divided and put in different sections.

First we should already be cognizant of the word *person* so no explanation is needed here, but the second word to appear in the phrase is of definite importance and that is the word *include*.

This is another contentious word in law and there has been great confusion in its use. So it is necessary to clarify this word before we can go on with our deconstruction. I think most people believe *include* means to become a part of something, as I did at one point, but this is just the common usage. To give an example of a dictionary definition *include* means

To confine within; to hold; to contain; to shut up; to enclose;.[67]

What we see here is the real meaning, which is why we say that it means to become a part of something, because the true meaning is 'to confine within.' So

---

[63] Ibid, Section 6

[64] Ibid, Section 5

[65] Ibid, Schedule 1

[66] Interpretation Act 1889 taken from Stroud's Judicial Dictionary

[67] "include." *Webster's Revised Unabridged Dictionary*. MICRA, Inc. 01 Jul. 2009.

when someone includes you in an activity you become confined within that activity, which is another way of saying to become a part of something.

In law the word *include* uses its original meaning, as in 'to confine within,' thus when used in a statute it is not the same as ordinary usage. This is one of the fundamental guides to statutory construction and interpretation, which are expressed in a famous maxim;

Expressio unius est exclusio alterius (The express mention of one thing excludes all others)

It must be understood that this is a guide to construction and not a rule to follow obediently. Saying that it does provide light onto the word *include*. If we were to follow the wisdom of the maxim and see the connection to the standard meaning of the word *include*, we can gain a better understanding. Or as Bennion states:

"The expressio unius principle is also applied where a formula which in itself may or may not include a certain class is accompanied by words of extension naming only some members of that class. The remaining members of the class are then taken to be excluded"[68]

For example by applying the above maxim to the phrase *"Person includes a body of persons corporate or unincorporate"* we could say that by expressing that a *person* is '*a body of persons corporate or unincorporate,'* which would only imply *legal person* and naturally excludes the *natural person*. For if we remember in law the word *person* refers to a certain class.

The other way of saying this is by using the standard definition of *include*, meaning to confine within, to hold or contain, to shut up to enclose. The phrase '*Person includes a body of persons corporate or unincorporate,'* would be interpreted as that *person* is only *a body of persons corporate or unincorporate,* for the usage is confined within the word, enclosed by the very word *include*. Nothing else may enter it.

So by clarifying the word *include* then it can be implied that *person* in the interpretation act would appear to exclude *natural persons* and only refer to *legal persons*. Now this is interesting because if you look back to the 1889 interpretation act, that phrase which was moved in the 1978 act, '*unless the contrary intention appears,'* would seem to indicate that if a statute referred to the *natural person* this would be the appearance of the contrary intention. Therefore *person from 1889 to 1978* and to date would have appeared only to refer to *legal persons* unless the phrase *natural person* appeared.

---

[68] Bennion on Statute Law by Francis Bennion, Published Longman, 1990, p.201

It has been argued that the word *include* is expansive, but this comes from the common usage, for if you keep including things into something else expansion occurs. Many legal scholars try to press forth this point that seems to go against the very words they use. For example Wilberforce states that

"...it has been considered that the Legislature has intentionally given words a more extended meaning than they would ordinarily receive. The interpretation clause sometimes provides that a certain word shall " include" a variety of things, and it is then held that this phrase is used by way of extension, and not as giving a definition by which other things are to be excluded."[69]

However In the very Interpretation Act of 1978, it specifically gives a list of definitions under schedule 1[70] in the act. The title being 'Words and phrases defined,' you will see many definitions because it will say something like "this means that." But in three or four cases it uses the words include, like is the case with the word *person*. Now if Wilberforce is right then by using the word *include* it does not give a definition, yet schedule 1 explicitly states that these are words and phrases defined. If it were a true defintion then our contentious phrase would look more like this:

"Person means a body of persons corporate or unincorporate."

Let us try and apply this idea of expansion to an ordinary sentence, e.g. *'dinner includes roast beef and roast potatoes.'* The word dinner is to mean a type of meal, so really it is like our word *person*, a class of things and not a thing in itself. Therefore a real defintion of the word dinner would be 'a meal eaten at night.' If we use the word *include* then we are not defining the word dinner but describing the constituent parts. So our example above basically states that dinner will consist of roast beef and roast potatoes. It does not expand on the meaning but elucidates the contents, therefore it only expands on what parts of a class of things are going to be used in the meaning. Now there are many foods which could make up a dinner so the need to elucidate the contents is necessary, but for the class of persons we only have two constituents, namely *natural persons* and *legal persons*. By this reasoning then the word *include* is not expansive but descriptive. So when we see the a word followed by include we are dealing with a class of things and what comes after that is restricting the use of the word to what is elucidated. If we were to use the reasoning of the judiciary on the word *include* then a phrase like 'dinner includes peas' would mean that dinner means every type of food plus peas.

---

[69] Statute law by Edward Wilberforce, 1881, Stevens and son, p. 299
[70] See Appendix c, Schedule 1

But there are times that the phrase *'includes but not limited to'*[71] will appear in a statute, which also seems to suggest that *include* is a word of limitation and not expansion. Another way of saying what *include* means might be to say that *'include is used with the intention of saying.'* For we must reiterate our own maxim for meaning which was:

> *"The word is not the thing it represents but gets its meaning from its use"*

This small definition given to us by the 1978 Interpretation act seems full of contradictions, for even if we look up the word *definition* we see that it means:

> *"The act of defining or making definite, distinct, or clear"*[72]

Now if we look once again to the 1978 acts definition would this be even called a definition?

> *"Person includes a body of persons corporate or unincorporate"*[73]

Clearly by using the same word to define itself is surely not the essence of clarity or distinction, not to mention the opposite of definite, which means:

> *"...clearly defined or determined; not vague or general; fixed; precise; exact"*[74]

Vagueness seems to sum up the 1978 acts definition of *person*. Now in every act of parliament the word *person* is to be construed as how they have stated it in the 1978 Interpretation act. So this vagueness spread through the thousands of acts that the word *person* appears in multiple times. Could it not have been easier just to say that *person* includes *natural persons* and *legal persons?* There is another maxim of law that would seem to cover the state of affairs we see before us, which is.

> *"It is a miserable slavery where the law is vague or uncertain.(Misera est servitus, ubi jus est vagum aut incertum.)"*

Is this not what we see before us, the law being uncertain and vague, and does the current state of affairs reflect this? This is up to the reader to ascertain, for where one person agrees another may not.

Let us now look into the rest of the phrase *'a body of persons corporate or unincorporate'* to conclude our deconstruction. The first word that strikes us here is the term *body*, but since it is being used idiomatically in the term *'a body*

---

[71] Examples of this can be seen in such acts as the data protection act; freedom of information act;

[72] http://dictionary.reference.com/browse/definition

[73] Interpretation Act 1978 (c.30), Schedule 1

[74] http://dictionary.reference.com/browse/definite

of persons' we must look towards the idiom rather than the separate words. For then it would mean *'as a group; together; collectively*[75] or *'A group of individuals regarded as an entity.'*[76] So we have a group of *persons* and if we refer back to our definition of *person* form the last part.

Person – *An entity with the ability or capacity to have rights and duties*

We seem to have a group of entities with the ability or capacity to have rights and duties which is amended by the phrase corporate or incorporate. Now as should be known by now that a body corporate can be either a corporation aggregate or corporation sole.

Unincorporate just means they haven't been incorporated and thus can mean associations, like charities or member interest clubs or things or their ilk. And have separate characteristics, elucidated below

"An unincorporated association:

- *is not a legal entity,*
- *is an organisation of persons or bodies (more than one) with an identifiable membership (possibly changing),*
- *has a membership who are bound together for a common purpose by an identifiable constitution or rules (which may be written or oral),*
- *is an organisation where the form of association is not one which is recognised in law as being something else (for example, an incorporated body or a partnership),*
- *must have an existence distinct from those persons who would be regarded as its members,*
- *The tie between the persons need not be a legally enforceable contract."*[77]

So by this deconstruction can we not give a more distinct clarification of the definition of *person* in the 1978 Act. The original definition was:

"Person includes a body of persons corporate or unincorporate."

Our definition would go something like this:

"Person is used with the intention of saying that it refers to a group of entities with the ability or capacity to have rights and duties, namely corporations'

---

[75] http://dictionary.reference.com/browse/body
[76] Ibid
[77] http://www.hmrc.gov.uk/manuals/ctmanual/ctm41305.htm

aggregate and unincorporated associations (who do not possess any legal personality)

Now this a lot more complex of an explanation but it gives you an idea of how the interpretation act is trying to define the word *person*. Our definition was meant to provide more clarity; well to some extent it clarifies what the 1978 Interpretation Act is trying to say. But we do not get much clarity for a layperson's understanding. For this we can call it vague and misleading and the consequences of this can be profound.

It is generally assumed that because the word *person* refers to a human being as most people use it, but as we have shown this is not strictly true. In the second part of this work we described the word *person* as a class of things in law. Now it should be up to the 1978 Interpretation Act to say what it includes in that class, and nowhere do you see a natural person. Of course, they will say it is naturally implied because of ordinary usage. This is not the case in law, for the ordinary usage of *person* is completely different from the legal usage. Of we were to take their idea that *person* is implied, then how do we know when it refers to the *natural person* or when it refers the *legal person*? Can you not see the vagueness and generality of their use of the word *person?* Therefore it is a truly miserable slavery we live under with such absurdities in these laws which control our lives.

However to understand this absurdity we must look closer into how a statute is constructed and therefore interpreted. For this lies at the heart of the problem with our word *person*, because of the regularity it is used with we must understand the framework it derives its context.

This, understandably, will be the most difficult part of this work as statutory construction and interpretation is a very technical art form, yet an attempt will be made to make it more intelligible to the reader. For if it is difficult for the people whose job it is to draft these statutes, then for the common man it must be nearly impossible. For as Bennion, one of the leading authorities on statutory interpretation, says

"Modern statute law consists of a set of written texts which (in themselves) are difficult to understand if you are a lawyer and impossible if you are not. Yet misapprehension will not avail as a shield: ignorantia juris non excusat."[78]

The Latin maxim he quotes means simply ignorance of the law is no excuse. Which for us common folk simply means that it's not their fault if you don't understand the law; you only have yourself to blame. So seemingly in the eyes of law we must know the essence of what law is, every statute and know what it all means.

---

[78] Bennion on Statute Law by Francis Bennion, Published Longman, 1990, p.10

If this was true then what need is there for the legal profession, for if we have to know everything then they would not be necessary.

Statutory Construction and Interpretation

We must make a clear difference between the construction of a statute and the interpretation of it. The construction of a statute is usually drafted by someone of the legal profession expressing the will of parliament. The interpretation is to aid those who adjudicate the law.

To go too deeply into the construction of statues is not too necessary in this work, but some references from time to time will be necessary. The more important and relevant to our argument is how the law is interpreted, thus we will look into some general themes of how a statute must be interpreted.

The English language must be one of the languages of the world most open to interpretation, and in essence this is highly subjective, which those who adjudicate the law have found out. It is said that nine out of every cases that reach the House of Lords, the highest court of appeal, deals with statutory interpretation. So you can see this is an important topic, especially in the context of this work. However because this has been such a problem some guidelines have, over time, been developed to aid in the interpretation of statutes, which we will give a brief sketch of now.

There are many aids that a judge can fall back on. The four primary ones are succintly described below.

The Mischief Rule

One of the original purposes of Statute Law was to provide a remedy where the common law did not cover. This rule lets the judge look at the former state of the law to find out the mischief the statute was meant to remedy.[79]

---

[79] Backed by Heydon's Case [1584] EWHC Exch J36 (01 January 1584), *Smith v Hughes* (1960), *Corkery v Carpenter* (1951)

The Golden Rule

The golden rule states that if there is any ambiguity in the interpretation of a word then to avoid absurdity the court must adopt an interpretation to avoid this.[80]

The Literal Rule

The literal rule[81] was given by Lord Esher in the famous case of '*R v Judge of the City of London Court* (1892)' in which he said

>*"If the words of an Act are clear then you must follow them even though they lead to a manifest absurdity. The court has nothing to do with the question whether the legislature has committed an absurdity."*[82]

This basically sums up the literal rule quite nicely.

The Purposive Approach

The purposive approach[83] is to find out the intent of parliament when it drafted the legislation. It must me pointed out that this is one of the more controversial aids to interpretation. For it has beeen said that:

>*"the purposive approach is one used by most continental European countries when interpreting their own legislation. It is also the approach which is taken by the European Court of Justice in interpreting EU law."*[84]

These are the four main guides by which judges interprate the law, however there are more aids that the ajudicators can fall back on. For there are rules of langauge, in the form of maxims, and external and intrinic aids. These other aids are more specific than the general rules laid out before.

The rules of language are like the maxim '*Expressio unius est exclusio alterius*' we introduced before the other two popular ones area as follows:

---

[80] Backed by Adler v George *(1964)*, Re Sigsworth *(1935)*
[81] Backed by *Whiteley v Chappell* (1868), *London & North Eastern Railway v Berriman* (1946)
[82] http://www.peterjepson.com/law/legislation_cases.htm
[83] Backed by *Notham v London Borough of Barnet* (1978), *Royal College of Nursing v DHSS* (1980), *Jones v Tower Boot Co Ltd* (1997)
[84] http://openlearn.open.ac.uk/mod/resource/view.php?id=208918&direct=1

Ejusdem generis

This literally means 'of the same kind,' which means any general word used after specific words it assumed that they are of the same class. For example if something included lions and tigers and other dangerous animals, animals like rabbits or cats would be exluded, as they are not dangerous animals.[85]

Noscitur a sociis

This maxim is used to mean 'a word is known by the company it keeps,' of course this is not the literal translation but its use in interpretation. Basically it means if a word is ambiguous then one must look at the context in which it is written i.e. the whole statute.[86]

Along with the *Expressio unius* these make the three primary maxims of interpretation

Next we turn to the intrinsic aids of interpretation, which apart form one thing will be found in the statute itself. The one thing that is outside of the statute is the Interpretation Act, which must be referred to. The parts in the statute whic are aids are the following

- The long title – this is to show the general objectives of the statute.
- The preamble – this was supposed to elucidate the mischief that the statute was to be the remedy for
- Interpretation sections – Most statutes have their own interpretation sections and they must be looked out if a different meaning is intended.
- Other things such as headings and sidenotes and explanatory sections (which is a recent occurence)

External aids on the other hand come from a variety of sources.

- Dictionaries – these are often used for finding the legal meaning of a word.
- Works by eminent writers such as Blackstone, Coke, Salmond, et al. Although these are not law itself they give a different but authoritive perspective to the law.
- Other cases are also an important aid in the interpretation of an act for if some judge has deemed a word to mean such and such, then many other judges follow the reasoning and use the interpretation.

---

[85] Backed by *Allen v Emerson* [1944] QBD, *Evans v Cross* (1938), *Powell v Kempton Park Racecourse* (1899)
[86] Backed by **Muir v Keay** (1875), *Inland Revenue Commissioners v Frere* [1964] HL

- Hansaard – these are the words of the house of prliament written down and are used to find out the intention of parliament. Before this was not allowed but know it is more acceptable.
- Official reports – writings from such organiations such as the law commision, the royal commision or other advisory bodies.

There are probably more extrenal aids but these cover the most important devices used in interpretation.

So now we have seen the help that is given to those who have to interpret the maze of words that make up a statute. This of course is a simplistic explanation and the reader must take this on board, but there are plenty of works in the public domain which go deeper into this subject. An overview is sufficient for this work.

So how do we relate this all back to the *person* in law? Well what we have seen so far is the origins and history of the the word, what the common usage of the word means, how law uses the word and finally how statute law regards the *person*. But the more contentious of what we have seen has to be how a *person* is regarded in statute law, since the "defintion" is really no defintion at all. when we refer back to how the law regards the *person*. So we now must look into the connection between Statute Law and the person. So can we apply some of these to the interpretation statute.

Statutory Interpretation and The Interpretation Act

So we have the following phrase:

"Person includes a body of persons corporate or unincorporate."

Can we now use some of the rules of interpretation and apply it to this contentious little phrase. We have already applied the *Expressio unius* rule and according to this our phrase excludes *natural persons*. We cannot use the *Ejusdem generis* rule because of the nature of the phrase, but we can use the other maxim of construction, *Noscitur a sociis*. With this maxim we must consider the whole statute in the interpretation of the definition of *person*. As we quoted above, which we will repeat again.

"In any Act, unless the contrary intention appears, words and expressions listed in Schedule 1 to this Act are to be construed according to that Schedule."

As you can see that all statutes must abide by the defintion of *person* unless the contrary appears. Now the schedule is entitled "words and expressions defined," which would indicate that the phrase that follows the word is the defintion. So by applying the *Noscitur a sociis* maxim any word under this schedule is a defintion whether or not they use the word 'include' or 'mean,' simply by the nature of the section.

Combine the *Noscitur a sociis* maxim with the *Expressio unius* rule and we have our word *person* to mean that it only refers to a *legal person*.

If we turn to our interperative aids developed by the judges, namely the mischief, golden, literal and purposive rules of interpretation.

Beginning with the mischief rule we can assume the interpretation act was meant to solidify the interpretation of statutes to get rid of the mischief of badly constructed statutes by giving some solid guidlines on the construction and interpretation of statutes. The reason that *person* is included in the definition is because there must have been controversy with the very word. We can see this clearly by our investigation carried out in part 2 of this work, as the *person* in law is not as simple as it seems. So it would seem to suggest that the inclusion of the word and its defintion was to remedy the mischief that was being caused by its misuse.

Now we must apply the Golden rule, 'if there is any ambiguity in the interpretation of a word then to avoid absurdity the court must adopt an interpretation to avoid this.' Well since the interpretation act was crafted to avoid any ambiguity, it would seem to be the embodiment of the golden rule, since statutes were meant to provide a remedy where common law provided none. What other interpretation are we supposed to take if, as mentioned above, the interpretation act states '"In any Act, unless the contrary intention appears, words and expressions listed in Schedule 1 to this Act are to be construed according to that Schedule.' All acts of parliament refer back to the interpretation act if there is any doubt. So the golden rule seems to indicate that the definition of *person* is the one to be found in the interpretation act.

If we now apply the literal rule to the defintion of person we just have to accept the interpretation act's defintion. So what we have is that the word *person* only refers to the *legal person* and bodies unincorporate. So any time in any act, unless the contrary appears, even of it leads to absurdity it must refer to a *legal person*. Of course this will lead to absurdity unless the legislature had some intention with this strange definition. But as the interpretations says 'unless the contrary appears,' so we must find the contrary, which would be mentioning the *natural person*. One of the most strange examples, of which there are few, is in the human rights act.

"Every natural or legal person is entitled to the peaceful enjoyment of his possessions"[87]

Well this is one mention of the natural person, which in the human rights act you might expèct to find. The strange thing is why is a legal person mentioned? For they are not human. A conundrum indeed! So if the definition of *person* in the interpretation included *natural persons* by implication then it would not be necessary to say it. There are more instances of the natural person being referred to, but they are few and far between.

When we turn to the purposive approach we must look to hansard to find the intentions of parliament to see what they say about the interpretation act. Unfortunatley there is very little reference to this clause in the 1978 act and only indirect references to the 1889 definition. As Mr Edmund Robertson says in one commitee session

"I have been asked, for instance, if a railway company is a public authority. I do not know whether it is meant to be included in "public authority or persons." "Person" would be included under the Interpretation Act, because railway companies under that Act are incorporations, and "person" includes incorporations. "Person," as I understand it, is either natural or artificial, and an artificial "person" is an incorporation. But all other groups of human beings who are not incorporated are simply collections of individuals"[88]

Or as MR. A. G. Murray says in the same session.

"I think the word "person," in the singular, would be sufficient, because, with the aid of the Interpretation Act, either in its natural sense or as relating to a body corporate or incorporate, it would include every body"[89]

And,

"The 19th Section of the Interpretation Act states that in every Act passed after that Act the expression "person" includes any body or person corporate or incorporate; and, so far as I know, there is no body which is not corporate or incorporate."[90]

These three examples show indirectly how the word person is interpretated by some. The problem here is that purposive approach seeks to find the intention of parliament but surely the act itself is the intent of parliament, or why would an act be written in such a way. The purposive approach is a slightly more contreversial approach as it seeks to imitate the continental approach to

---

[87] http://www.statutelaw.gov.uk, Human Rights Act 1998, schedule 1, part 2, article 1
[88] http://hansard.millbanksystems.com/commons/1899/jun/12/committee#S4V0072P0_18990612_HOC_158
[89] Ibid
[90] Ibid

interpretation, which are all, except us, civil law countries and so approach law in an entirely different way.

In part two we looked to some of the extrinsic aids, by saying what leading authorities have to say on the subject and the conclusion can be found there. What we are left with by using some aids of interpretation is some very contradictory views on what a *person* is in the 1978 Interpretation act. We have deconstructed the interpretation act and from that it seems that *person* only refers to the *legal person*. Also by applying some interpretative aids to the act most of the evidence seems to point towards the same conclusion that unless the contrary appears (as it does in the human rights act or the consumer credit act[91]) *person* refers to a *legal person*.

I think the question is that lies before us is why is the *natural person* excluded from the definition, if it is well known in the legal world that word *person* in legal knowledge refers to two different types. Would it not be easy to put these two simple words *"natural person"* in the 1978 interpretation act and clear up the ambiguity? For at that time the differemce between the legal and natural person was a well established idea in law. It does appear suspicious that such a simple thing has not been amended and such ambiguity has been allowed to continue, but this if this is the legislators will can there be a reason to leave the state of affairs as they are?

So after all that has been seen it is now time to find out the answer to our intial question, "Is a Human Being a person?"

[91] http://www.opsi.gov.uk/

Conclusion

Is a Human Being a Person?

Conclusion

Can we now begin to formulate an answer to our question? I think it would be wise to summarise our findings before we can begin to even suggest an answer. To show Greenbough and kittredge's diagram would help us give us a visual summary first.

1.	A	A mask
2.	A+B	character indicated by mask
3.	B	character or role in (play)
4.	B+C	one who represents a character
5.	C	a representative in general
6.	C+D	a representative of church in Parish
7.	D	a parson
8.	D+E	a parson with high rank or office
9.	E	someone with high rank or office
10.	E+F	high rank/office has status
11.	F	someone with status
12.	F+G	s/one with status has rights
13.	G	anyone with rights
14.	G+H	any entity with rights

In the first part of this work we looked at the history of the word *person* from which we found the original meaning was (A) in our diagram, simply a mask. Over the course of centuries this meaning transformed in to a character or role (B) which meaning or use we still retain in the word persona. This later morphed into a representative (C) as a character was representative of something. Our look into etymology then led us to see that at one point in our history the word *person* was synonymous with the word parson. Since the word *person* was related to parson and by extension parsonage and personage are related. Thus with the meaning taking on a religious connatation, status was introduced into the concepts (see E to F), this was naturally influenced by the power of the church and state at that time.

Next we looked at law and this gave our definitions F to G+H as a *person* and rights are intimately linked, one is irrelevant without the other. So by viewing this diagram we can see quickly and easily the evolution of the word, but the story doesn't end there, we are still left with our question of why we call a human being a person. Well this would become defintion H if we carried on our diagram, but we first must look at this more logically.

It is assumed that every Human Being has rights, naturally called Human rights, and this can be see in Appendix B in the three documents of rights which are applicable to us. And if we remember Salmonds quote above

"So far as legal theory is concerned, a person is any being whom the law regards as capable of rights and duties"

From this we can say that because all humans have rights and since law regards any being with rights as a person. Then logically all Human Beings are *persons*, syllogystically it would look like this

All Human Beings have rights

Rights only belong to persons (*Under law*)

Thus all human beings are persons

So to finish our diagram let us add definition H to see the final picture of the evolution of the word *person*.

1.	A			A mask
2.	A+B			character indicated by mask
3.	B			character or role in (play)
4.	B+C			one who represents a character
5.	C			a representative in general
6.	C+D			a representative of church in Parish
7.	D			a parson
8.	D+E			a parson with high rank or office
9.	E			someone with high rank or office
10.	E+F			high rank/office has status
11.	F			someone with status
12.	F+G			s/one with status has rights
13.	G			anyone with rights
14.	G+H			any entity with rights
15.	H			a human being

This would be seem the source of the concept that a Human Being is referred to as a *person*, because of the evolution of a word throughout the centuries and its adaptation into law. It was a slow process, full of iniquities, which has brought into the language a word which means one thing in one sphere of life and something different in another. Unfortunately these spheres, both law and ordinary life, do not exist separately. So we have to make distinction between these two spheres otherwise confusion is inevitable.

Common usage of the word *person* as a synonym of human being has no inherent difficulties, it is the laws adaptation of the word that has created the confusion and thus the necessity of this work. The creation of the *person* as a vehicle for rights was a slow process and whether this process is still continuing we cannot say, but we can say that a concept hundreds of years old is still being applied today. It is quite easy to say that not all persons are human beings, but rather difficult to say the contrary that not all human beings are persons, yet in many periods of history this has been the case.

However as we found out in Part 2 of this work that the word *person* in law actually referred to a class of things rather than a specific thing. Thus when we refer to a human being as a *person* we are in fact refering to a class humans belong to. An example of this would be similar to calling another human a mammal. Technically it is correct that all humans are mammals, but not all mammals are human beings, which is very much like the situation with the word *person*. So when we read the word *person* in any legislation it is referring to a class of beings in law, not the common usuage of the word, which has probably been adapted from law and not the other way round.

So what is the answer to our question? Is a Human Being a *person* or not? Unfortunately there is no straightforward answer, becuase we can both say yes and no, it is entirely dependent on certain conditions. When a human being is a *person* it is because they have the ability or capacity for rights, thus it is entirely dependent on the connection between rights and duties and the legal personality. Hypothetically speaking. if a human has no rights then they cannot be considered a *person*. Technically speaking, since a person is a class of things or beings then a human being is not a *person* and if we really want to be pedantic we are not human beings as this too is a class. We are a man or a woman, a male or a female, for this these are the true nouns for both sexes of our species.

It is because we have all these rights and duties attached to us that we are considered to be *persons* under the eyes of the law. The long struggle for human rights created, in law, a persona to which these rights belong, which we see mirrored in the concept of the *legal person*. This fictional entity has no physical existence yet it has the same rights and duties that every man and woman possesses. But this *legal person* exists in law equally the same as the physical man or woman, and since this is the case we can suggest that being a *person* has very little to do with physical existence but some metaphysical existence that law or society has created and maintains. If we were stretch this further it would seem that the law is the one that confers these rights and legal personality, neither being natural in its strictest sense. For we have seen in Appendix B the three fundamental human rights documents have been written to give all humans rights and because of this all men are *persons*. But can a human being reject these rights and duties and thus strip himself of his legal personality? Or is the process auotmatic the moment we are born?

What we have found out in this work is the central link between rights and the *person*, which in turn must be linked with the society and law a man lives in. However we must make a division between the common usuage of the word *person*, which is entirely different from the technical meaning in law. This is the point that must be understood and absorbed that words in different contexts are used in different ways. It is the hope of this work that people understand the difference and what this distinction implies in everyday life.

In Britain we have looked at the law and how the word *person* is used, but it is filled with ambiguity and confusion which the law abhors, which will naturally affect the common man. Whether this is intentional or unintentional it is not for me to say, but if one is aware of the difference in its use then it is a useful piece of knowledge for us to have when dealing with that are of life i.e. the law. It cannot be more strongly emphasised how the law affects our lives overtly and covertly. From birth we are under the eyes of law and it follows us to our death, so to not put importance of the effect of some of the smaller points of law that fly under the radar, just like our controversial word *person*, is unexcusable. As you should have seen by now in this work how the effect of one word has had on the evolution of our society, we should realise the effect it is producing now and in our daily lives.

It is up to the reader the importance that is put on this word, but hopefully you have a greater knowledge of our little friend and how it is used both in ordinary life and in law. What you do now with this information lies on the shoulder of the readers.

Bibliography

- Significant Etymology: by James Mitchell (1908), footnote, William Blackwood and Sons
- The theatre, its development in France and England, and a history of its Greek and Latin origins: by Charles Hastings (1901) Duckworth & Co
- Words and their ways in English speech: by Greenough and Kittridge, (1902). Macmillan and Co.
- Roman Britain by H.M. Scarth, London, S.P.C.K
- http://www.etymonline.com
- Analytical dictionary of the English language by David Booth, 1835, Cochrane and Co.
- As You Like It by William Shakespeare, 1599
- The Origins of Political Correctness An Accuracy in Academia Address by Bill Lind, 2000
- Political Correctness by Philip Atkinson, http://www.ourcivilisation.com/pc.htm

- George Orwell: 'Politics and the English Language' First published: *Horizon*. GB, London., April 1946
- Philosophical Investigations by Ludwig Wittgenstein, 1953, Basil Blackwell Ltd
- Science and Sanity by Alfred Korzybski, 5th Edition, Institute of General semantics, 1994,
- Jurisprudence and the law by John Salmond, second edition, Steven and Hayes, 1907,
- A first book of Jurisprudence, by Sir Frederick Pollock, second edition, 1904, Macmillian and Co
- Elements of Law by William Markby, sixth edition, Oxford press, 1905
- A Treatisse of Universal Jurisprudence by John Penford Thomas, second edition, 1829
- http://dictionary.reference.com

- *Commentaries on the Laws of England in Four Books by William Blackstone*, Philadelphia: J.B. Lippincott Co., 1893
- The Common Law, Oliver Wendell Holmes Jr., 1882, Macmillan and Co.
- A Treatise on the law relating to Municipal Corporations in England and Wales by Thomas Arnold, Third edition 1863
- The British citizen: His rights and priviliges, a short history, 1885, E. & J.B. Young
- A short history of women's rights, By Eugene Hecker, Second edition, 1914, G.P. Putman's sons
- An Elementary Commentary on English Law by Alfred Ruegg, 1920, George Allen & Unwin Ltd
- The history of the common law of england by Matthew Hale, 1820, sixth edition, Butterworths
- The Judicial Dictionary, by F.Stroud, 1903, Second Edition, Sweet and Maxwell Ltd
- Bennion on Statute Law by Francis Bennion, Published Longman, 1990
- Statute law by Edward Wilberforce, 1881, Stevens and son
- http://www.statutelaw.gov.uk
- http://hansard.millbanksystems.com
- http://www.opsi.gov.uk/

Appendix A

From Ballentines Law Dictionary, third edition

person. An individual or an organization. UCC § 1201(30). An individual man, woman, or child or, as a general rule, a corporation. 18 Am J2d Corp § 20. Inclusive of bodies politic and corporate. Waterbury v Board of Com. 10 Mont 515, 26 P 1002. As used in the Bankruptcy Act, inclusive of corporations, officers, partnerships, and women, except where otherwise specified. Bankruptcy Act § 1(23); 11 USC § 1(23). Under the negotiable Instruments Law, an individual or a body of persons whether incorporated or not. Uniform Negotiable Instruments Law § 191. As used in the anti-trust laws, inclusive of corporations and associations. 36 Am J1st Monop etc § 186. Inclusive of corporations where used in a statute imposing a license tax. 33 Am J1st Lic § 49. Usually inclusive of corporations in a tax statute, 51 Am J1st Tax § 318. Inclusive of corporations where used in a statute relating to the sale of commodities by weight or measure. 56 Am J1st W & L § 5. Inclusive of corporations in a pure food law. State v Belle Springs Creamery Co.

[940]

83 Kan 389, 111 P 474. For the purposes of the due process clause, either a citizen or an alien. 3 Am J2d Aliens § 8. For the purposes of extradition, either a citizen or an alien. 31 Am J2d Extrad § 17.

A corporation is deemed a "person" within the meaning of the statute of limitations, and consequently, the statute ordinarily runs against corporations and domestic corporations are generally included within the class of persons who may plead the statute, and they may, as a general rule, acquire title by adverse possession for the statutory period in the same manner and to the same extent as an individual. 34 Am J1st Lim Ac § 372. A municipal corporation is a "person" within the meaning of the statute of limitations. 34 Am J1st Lim Ac § 397.

Liquor license laws may either expressly permit, or be held susceptible of a construction which authorizes corporations to be licensed thereunder, and the word "person," as used in such legislation, is usually held to embrace a corporation, irrespective of whether there is an express provision to that effect in the license law or in general law. 30 Am J Rev ed Intox L § 126.

The word "person," where used in statutes defining crimes, is usually construed to include a corporation, so as to bring corporations within the prohibition of the statute. 19 Am J2d Corp § 1436.

Dependent upon the entire context of the instrument, the word "person," as used in a will, may or may not include a corporation. 57 Am J1st Wills § 1326.

From Black's law dictionary first edition

PERSON. A man considered according to the rank he holds in society, with all the rights to which the place he holds entitles him, and the duties which it imposes. 1 Bonv. Inst. no. 137.

A human being considered as capable of having rights and of being charged with duties; while a "thing" is the object over which rights may be exercised.

Persons are divided by law into **natural** and **artificial.** Natural persons are such as the God of nature formed us; artificial are such as are created and devised by human laws, for the purposes of society and government, which are called "corporations" or "bodies politic." 1 Bl. Comm. 123.

From Black's law dictionary Fourth edition

PERSON. A man considered according to the rank he holds in society, with all the right to which the place he holds entitles him, and the duties which it imposes. People v. R. Co., 134 N.Y. 506, 31 N.E. 873.

The word in its natural and usual signification includes women as well as men. Commonwealth v. Welosky, 276 Mass. 398, 177 N.E. 656.

Term may include artificial beings, as corporations, 1 Bla.Com. 123; 4 Bingh. 669; People v. Com'rs of Taxes, 23 N.Y. 242; *quasi*-corporations, Sedgw. Stat. & Const. L. 372; L. R. 5 App. Cas. 857; territorial corporations, Seymour v. School District, 53 Conn. 507, 3 A. 552; and foreign corporations, People v. McLean, 80 N.Y. 259; under statutes, forbidding the taking of property without due process of law and giving to all persons the equal protection of the laws, Smyth v. Ames, 18 S.Ct. 418, 169 U.S. 466, 42 L.Ed. 819; Gulf, C. & S. F. R. Co. v. Ellis, 17 S.Ct. 255, 165 U.S. 150, 41 L.Ed. 666; concerning claims arising from Indian depredations, U. S. v. Transp. Co., 17 S.Ct. 206, 164 U.S. 686, 41 L.Ed. 599; relating to taxation and the revenue laws, People v. McLean, 80 N.Y. 254; to attachments, Bray v. Wallingford, 20 Conn. 416; usurious contracts, Philadelphia Loan Co. v. Towner, 13 Conn. 249; applying to limitation of actions, Olcott v. R. Co., 20 N.Y. 210, 75 Am.Dec. 393; North Mo. R. Co. v. Akers, 4 Kan. 453, 96 Am.Dec. 183; and concerning the admissibility as a witness of a party in his own behalf when the opposite party is a living person, La Farge v. Ins. Co., 22 N.Y. 352. A corporation is also a person under a penal statute; U. S. v. Amedy, 11 Wheat. 392, 6 L.Ed. 502. Corporations are "persons" as that word is used in the first clause of the XIVth Amendment; Covington & L. Turnp. Co. v. Sandford, 17 S.Ct. 198, 164 U.S. 578, 41 L.Ed. 560; Smyth v. Ames, 18 S.Ct. 418, 169 U.S. 466, 42 L.Ed. 819; People v. Fire Ass'n, 92 N.Y. 311, 44 Am.Rep. 380; U. S. v. Supply Co., 30 S.Ct. 15, 215 U.S. 50, 54 L.Ed. 87; *contra*, Central P. R. Co. v. Board, 60 Cal. 35. But a corporation of another state is not a "person" within the jurisdiction of the state until it has complied with the conditions of admission to do business in the state, Fire Ass'n of Phila. v.

Continued On next page

New York, 7 S.Ct. 108, 119 U.S. 110, 30 L.Ed. 342; and a statutory requirement of such conditions is not in conflict with the XIVth Amendment; Pembina Consol. S. M. & M. Co. v. Pennsylvania, 8 S.Ct. 737, 125 U.S. 181, 189, 31 L.Ed. 650.

It may include partnerships. In re Julian, D. C.Pa., 22 F.Supp. 97, 99. Also firms. State ex rel. Joseph R. Peebles Sons Co. v. State Board of Pharmacy, 127 Ohio St. 513, 189 N.E. 447, 448.

"Persons" are of two kinds, natural and artificial. A natural person is a human being. Artificial persons include a collection or succession of natural persons forming a corporation; a collection of property to which the law attributes the capacity of having rights and duties. The latter class of artificial persons is recognized only to a limited extent in our law. Examples are the estate of a bankrupt or deceased person. Hogan v. Greenfield, 58 Wyo. 13, 122 P.2d 850, 853.

It has been held that when the word person is used in a legislative act, natural persons will be intended unless something appear in the context to show that it applies to artificial persons. Blair v. Worley, 1 Scam., Ill., 178; Appeal of Fox, 112 Pa. 337; 4 A. 149; but as a rule corporations will be considered persons within the statutes unless the intention of the legislature is manifestly to exclude them. Stribbling v. Bank, 5 Rand., Va., 132.

A county is a person in a legal sense. Lancaster Co. v. Trimble, 34 Neb. 752, 52 N.W. 711; but a sovereign is not; In re Fox, 52 N.Y. 535, 11 Am.Rep. 751; U. S. v. Fox, 94 U.S. 315, 24 L.Ed. 192, but confra within the meaning of a statute, providing a penalty for the fraudulent alteration of a public record with intent that any "person" be defrauded, Martin v. State, 24 Tex. 61; and within the meaning of a covenant for quiet and peaceful possession against all and every person or persons; Giddings v. Holter, 19 Mont. 263, 48 P. 8. An Indian is a person, U. S. v. Crook, 5 Dill. 459, Fed.Cas.No.14,891; and a slave was so considered, in so far, as to be capable of committing a riot in conjunction with white men, State v. Thackam, 1 Bay, S.C., 358. The estate of a decedent is a person, Billings v. State, 107 Ind. 54, 6 N.E. 914, 7 N.E. 763, 57 Am. Rep. 77; and where the statute makes the owner of a dog liable for injuries to any person, it includes the property of such person, Brewer v. Crosby, 11 Gray, Mass., 29; but where the statute provided damages for the bite of a dog which had previously bitten a person, it was held insufficient to show that the dog had previously bitten a goat, [1896] 2 Q.B. 109; a dog will not be included in the word in an act which authorizes a person to kill dogs running at large, Helsrodt v. Hackett, 34 Mich. 283, 22 Am.Rep. 529.

Where the statute prohibited any person from pursuing his usual vocation on the Lord's Day, it was held to apply to a judge holding court. Bass v. Irvin, 49 Ga. 436.

A child en ventre sa mere is not a person. Dietrich v. Northampton, 138 Mass. 14, 52 Am.Rep. 242; but an infant is so considered; Madden v. Springfield, 131 Mass. 441.

In the United States bankrupty act of 1898, it is provided that the word "persons" shall include corporations, except where otherwise specified, and officers, partnerships, and women, and, when used with reference to the commission of acts which are therein forbidden, shall include persons who are participants in the forbidden acts, and the agents, officers, and members of the board of directors or trustees, or their controlling bodies, of corporations. 11 U.S.C.A. ¶ 1.

Persons are the subject of rights and duties; and, as a subject of a right, the person is the object of the correlative duty, and conversely. The subject of a right has been called by Professor Holland, the person of inherence; the subject of a duty, the person of incidence. "Entitled" and "bound" are the terms in common use in English and for most purposes they are adequate. Every full citizen is a person; other human beings, namely, subjects who are not citizens, may be persons. But not every human being is necessarily a person, for a person is capable of rights and duties, and there may well be human beings having no legal rights, as was the case with slaves in English law.
* * *

A person is such, not because he is human, but because rights and duties are ascribed to him. The person is the

legal subject or substance of which the rights and duties are attributes. An individual human being considered as having such attributes is what lawyers call a natural person. Pollock. First Book of Jurispr. 110. Gray, Nature and Sources of Law, ch. II.

PERSONA. Lat.

In the civil law. Character, in virtue of which certain rights belong to a man and certain duties are imposed upon him. Thus one man may unite many characters, (personæ,) as, for example, the characters of father and son, of master and servant. Mackeld.Rom.Law, § 129.

In Ecclesiastical Law. The rector of a church instituted and inducted, for his own life, was called "persona mortalis;" and any collegiate or conventual body, to whom the church was forever appropriated, was termed "persona immortalis." Jacob.

PERSONA CONJUNCTA ÆQUIPARATUR IN-TERESSE PROPRIO. A personal connection [literally, a united person, union with a person] is equivalent to one's own interest; nearness of blood is as good a consideration as one's own interest. Bac.Max. 72, reg.

PERSONA DESIGNATA. A person pointed out or described as an individual, as opposed to a person ascertained as a member of a class, or as filling a particular character.

PERSONA ECCLESIÆ. The parson or personation of the church.

PERSONA EST HOMO CUM STATU QUODAM CONSIDERATUS. A person is a man considered with reference to a certain status. Heinecc. Elem. l. 1, tit. 3, § 75.

PERSONA NON GRATA. In international law and diplomatic usage, a person not acceptable (for reasons peculiar to himself) to the court or government to which it is proposed to accredit him in the character of an ambassador or minister.

PERSONA REGIS MERGITUR PERSONA DU-CIS. Jenk.Cent. 160. The person of duke merges in that of king.

PERSONA STANDI IN JUDICIO. Capacity of standing in court or in judgment; capacity to be a party to an action; capacity or ability to sue.

PERSONABLE. Having the rights and powers of a person; able to hold or maintain a plea in court; also capacity to take anything granted or given.

PERSONÆ VICE FUNGITUR MUNICIPIUM ET DECURIA. Towns and boroughs act as if persons. Warner v. Beers, 23 Wend., N.Y., 103, 144.

PERSONAL. Appertaining to the person; belonging to an individual; limited to the person; having the nature or partaking of the qualities of human beings, or of movable property. In re Steimes' Estate, 150 Misc. 279, 270 N.Y.S. 339.

As to personal "Action," "Assets," "Chattels," "Contract," "Covenant," "Credit," "Demand," "Disability," "Franchise," "Injury," "Judgment,"

From the Judicial and Statutory definitions of words and phrases, second edition.

PERSISTENCE—PERSIST

To satisfy the proviso of the Act of 1792 (3 Smith's Laws Pa. p. 73), "persistence," in the settlement of public land to save its forfeiture, "must mean something real; not merely the wishing or even attempting to do an act impossible, or so dangerous that no man could be expected to attempt it." Such proviso only dispenses with the forfeiture incurred, according to the law, by not making a settlement and continuing it, within and during the time prescribed by the enacting clause, and requires that it must be made as soon as the prevention ceases. Huldekoper v. Burrus, 12 Fed. Cas. 6848, pp. 840, 843, 1 Wash. 109, 118.

PERSON

See Artificial Persons; Colored Person; Credible Person; Disorderly Person; Existing Person; From the Person; Great Many Persons; Guardian of the Person; Injury to Person and Property; In Person; Larceny from the Person; Natural Person; No Person; Plea to the Person; Poor Person; Private Person; Proper Person; Prudent Person; Qualified Persons; Suitable Person; Suspicious Person; Third Person; White Person; With Every Other Person.

All persons, see All.

Any other person, see Any Other.

Any person, see Any.

Any person interested, see Any.

Every person, see Every.

Exposure of the person, see Exposure.

Other persons, see Other.

Such person, see Such.

As used in the statute limiting actions upon the penal statutes, where the penalty goes to the state, or county, or "person" suing for the same, the word "person" means simply any person who sues as a common informer and not one having a special interest by reason of any injury or grievance. Nebraska Nat. Bank v. Walsh, 59 S. W. 952, 953, 68 Ark. 436, 82 Am. St. Rep. 301.

The word "person," as used in Act Cong. July 1, 1903, c. 1362, § 22, 32 Stat. 643 providing that, if any person whose name appears on the rolls shall die before receiving his allotment the land to which he would have been entitled shall be allotted in his name, etc., includes members, citizens, and freedmen. Hancock v. Mutual Trust Co., 103 Pac. 566, 569, 24 Okl. 391.

Construed in plural

The word "person," as provided by Ky. St. § 457, may extend and be applied to persons. Commonwealth v. Adams Express Co., 97 S. W. 386, 387, 123 Ky. 720.

The word "person," as used in Laws 1901, p. 61, c. 62, § 1, imposing an inheritance tax upon property passing by will or the statutes of inheritance to any person in trust or otherwise, though importing the singular, includes the plural. Dixon v. Ricketts, 72 Pac. 947, 949, 26 Utah, 215.

The word "person," as used in the statutes relating to railroad commissioners, includes persons (Gen. St. 1901, § 5997). Kansas City, Outer Belt & Electric R. Co. v. Board of Railroad Com'rs, 84 Pac. 755, 756, 73 Kan. 168.

Rev. St. § 1024, provides that when there are several charges against any person for the same act or transaction, or for two or more connected acts or transactions, or for two or more acts or transactions in the same class of crimes or offenses, which may be properly joined, instead of having several indictments, the whole may be joined in one indictment in several counts; and, if two or more indictments are found, in such case the court may order them to be consolidated. Held, that under section 1, providing that words importing the singular number may apply to several persons or things, section 1024 was not limited to indictments against a single person, but embraced consolidated indictments against several defendants. Emanuel v. United States, 196 Fed. 317, 320, 116 C. C. A. 137.

Rev. St. c. 23, § 68, relating to ways, provides that when a way is changed in grade by a road commissioner or "person authorized," to the injury of an abutting owner, he may apply in writing to the municipal officers for an assessment of damages occasioned thereby to be paid by the town. Chapter 53, § 19, relating to street railroads, provides that such road shall be constructed and maintained in such manner and upon such grades as the municipal officers of the towns where they are located may direct, and when, in the judgment of such corporation, it shall be necessary to alter the grade of any road the alteration shall be made at the expense of the corporation in accordance with the directions of the municipal officers. Held, that the two sections should be construed together, and under Rev. St. c. 1, § 2, rules 2 and 14, by which the word "person" may include a corporation and singular words include plural, where a grade was established by municipal officers at the request of a railroad company, it must be deemed to have been done by a "person authorized" within the meaning of section 68, and though section 68 provides that the damages shall be assessed by the municipal officers to be paid by the town, and section 19, that the alterations shall be at the expense of the corporation, yet the word "expense" in section 19 will include the damages to landowners, which, if paid by the town, are a part of the expense of the alteration, and are recoverable by the town from the railroad corporation. Hurley v. Inhabitants of South Thomaston, 74 Atl. 734, 736, 105 Me. 301.

Construed as witness

Under Bankr. Act July 1, 1898, c. 541, § 41, 30 Stat. 556, providing that certain acts committed by any "person" before a referee in bankruptcy shall constitute a contempt of court, the word "person" is not limited to the bankrupt, but extends to a witness guilty of perjury before the referee. In re Bronstein, 182 Fed. 349, 353.

Code Civ. Proc. § 870, provides for the examination of a party, and section 871 authorizes the examination of a "person not a party" to the action. Held, that the word "person" in section 871 means a person who can testify as a witness; and hence such section did not authorize the examination of officers of a corporation before trial, where the corporation was not a party. Chartered Bank of India, Australia, and China v. North River Ins. Co., 121 N. Y. Supp. 399, 400, 136 App. Div. 646.

Bankrupt

Bankr. Act 1898, § 29b, provides that a "person" shall be punished by imprisonment on conviction of having concealed property belonging to his estate in bankruptcy. Section 1, cl. 19, provides that "persons" shall include corporations, except where otherwise specified. A careful reading of this clause, in connection with the terms of section 29b, convinces that it can have no effect to extend the terms or broaden the true interpretation of the latter subsection. All who are punishable under this subsection 29b are persons who are or who have been bankrupts. Hence none of those whom the word "persons" is made to include under section 1, cl. 19—no officers, partnerships, women, participants in forbidden acts, agents, officers, or members of any board of directors or trustees—can be guilty of the offense specified in this subsection, unless they are either bankrupts when they conceal the property or have been such and have obtained their discharges before that time. Present or past bankruptcy is an essential attribute of every person who may be an offender under this statute. Field v. United States, 137 Fed. 6, 7, 69 C. C. A. 568.

Bankr. Act July 1, 1898, c. 541, § 29b, 30 Stat. 554, provides that a person shall be punished on conviction of having concealed, while a bankrupt, or after his discharge, from his trustee, any of the property belonging to his estate. Held, that though there can be no offense unless the concealment is accomplished while there is a person in bankruptcy, or after his discharge, not only the bankrupt, but others aiding and abetting in the concealment, are punishable. United States v. Young & Holland Co., 170 Fed. 110–112.

Body of persons

The provisions of section 2134, Code Civ. Proc., directing that "each person upon whom a writ of certiorari is served * * * must make a return," etc., is not in conflict with the view that the return of a body or board may be made by a majority of its members, because the noun "person" is clearly used to denote any person or legal entity to whom a writ is directed. People ex rel. Lester v. Eno, 68 N. E. 868, 870, 176 N. Y. 513.

The use of the word "person" in Const. U. S. Amend. 14, providing that no state shall deprive any person of life, liberty, or property, without due process of law, includes the natural persons who compose a corporation, and who are the beneficial owners of all its property, the technical and legal title to which is in the corporation. State v. Atlantic Coast Line R. Co., 47 South. 969, 982, 56 Fla. 617, 32 L. R. A. (N. S.) 639.

In view of Rev. St. 1909, § 10,160, defining the word "persons" as including a body of persons whether incorporated or not, under sections 2528 and 3881, respectively, providing that if any person disobey an injunction, the circuit court to which it is returned, or any judge in vacation thereof, shall issue an attachment for the contempt, and that every court of record shall have power to punish as for criminal contempt, persons guilty of willful disobedience of any order, the circuit court has power to punish a corporation for civil contempt. Fiedler v. Bambrick Bros. Const. Co., 142 S. W. 1111, 1116, 162 Mo. App. 528.

Carrier

Code 1897, § 2419, provides that if any common carrier or person, or any one as agent or employé thereof, shall transport any person within the state any intoxicating liquors without first being furnished with a certificate that the consignee is the holder of a permit to sell intoxicating liquors in the county to which the shipment is made, such carrier or person shall on conviction be fined, etc. Held, that the word "person," as used in such section, means a public or private carrier, and did not include one who transported several interstate shipments of liquor from the railroad company's depot to the consignee's place of residence as a mere gratuity. State v. Wignall, 128 N. W. 935, 937, 150 Iowa, 650, 34 L. R. A. (N. S.) 507.

Children

The word "person," as used in a statute forbidding persons to walk along railroad tracks, should not be construed to include children so young as to be incapable of contributory negligence, under the rule that where a statute seeks to change an existing status of a portion of a community, the change must be made in language so clear as to unmistakably manifest such legislative purpose. Erie R. Co. v. Swiderski, 197 Fed. 521, 524, 117 C. C. A. 17.

Citizen

The word "persons" in the extradition treaty between the United States and Italy, entered into in 1868 (15 Stat. 629) and amended in 1884 (24 Stat. 1001), providing for the surrender of persons charged with enumerated crimes, is sufficiently broad to embrace citizens and subjects of the contracting parties, and a citizen of the United States, who while in Italy commits an offense, and who then flees to the United States, is within the treaty and may be extradited thereunder, though Italy has always construed the word so as not to include its citizens and subjects. Ex parte Charlton, 185 Fed. 880, 884.

Custom officer

Section 5445, Rev. St., relating to "every person" who aids in effecting the illegal entry of imports, while ordinarily not intended to apply to those individuals (customs officers) covered by the preceding section of the law, does not exclude an officer of the service if the facts bring him within the definition of the "person" at whom this provision is aimed, and may therefore include a customs weigher who aids in the way prohibited. United States v. Mescall, 164 Fed. 587, 588.

Deceased person or estate of deceased person

A corpse is not a "person." That which constitutes a person is separated from the body by death. Brooks v. Boston & N. St. Ry. Co., 97 N. E. 760, 211 Mass. 277.

A "person" includes a corporation and a joint-stock company, but it does not include an estate, or where an action is brought by the representative of an estate or trust as such; for the estate or the trust, and not the person who represents it, is really the party. Cole v. Manson, 85 N. Y. Supp. 1011, 42 Misc. Rep. 149.

Primary Election Law (Laws 1903, c. 451) § 18, subd. 1, provides that the person receiving the greatest number of votes at a primary as the candidate of a party for an office shall be the candidate of that party for such office, and his name as such candidate shall be placed on the official ballot at the following election. Held, that a dead man is not a "person" within the statute; such word meaning a living human being. State ex rel. Bancroft v. Frear, 128 N. W. 1068, 1071, 144 Wis. 79, 140 Am. St. Rep. 992.

Laws 1904, No. 30, § 81, provides that certain sections pertaining to taxes upon persons receiving property passing from decedents shall also apply to all "persons" dying before the passage of the act, but whose estates shall not have been at that time decreed or distributed, etc. Held, that "persons" refers to decedents mentioned in that section, and not to the beneficiaries. In re Howard's Estate, 68 Atl. 513, 514, 80 Vt. 489.

Where a wife loaned her husband money which was made payable on demand, and they both died without the wife having demanded, or received the money, her estate was a creditor of his estate, and a "person" within Rev. St. 1898, § 3840, providing for an order within which creditors shall present their claims and section 3844, providing that every person having a claim, who shall not, after notice given, exhibit it within the time limited, shall be forever barred. Barry v. Minahan, 107 N. W. 488, 491, 127 Wis. 570.

Employé

A mere ticket taker at a theater is not within Pen. Code, § 290, providing for the punishment of any "person" who admits to any theater, museum, or skating rink, or any place where wines or liquors are kept, any child under the age of 16 years, unless accompanied by its parent or guardian. People ex rel. Jacques v. Sheriff of Kings County, 106 N. Y. Supp. 387, 54 Misc. Rep. 8.

Forwarding agent

A forwarding agent is a "person" within the meaning of Interstate Commerce Act Feb. 4, 1887, c. 104, § 2, 24 Stat. 379, forbidding preferences and discrimination in rates. Interstate Commerce Commission v. Delaware, L. & W. R. Co., 31 Sup. Ct. 392, 396, 220 U. S. 235, 55 L. Ed. 448.

Infant or minor

A child of immature and tender years is a "person," within Rev. Codes N. D. 1905, § 7686, authorizing an action for the death of a "person" by the wrongful act of another. Scherer v. Schlaberg, 122 N. W. 1000, 1006, 18 N. D. 421, 24 L. R. A. (N. S.) 520.

Under the bankruptcy act providing that any natural person may be adjudged an involuntary bankrupt, the word "person" does not include an infant. In re Kehler, 153 Fed. 235, 237.

Bankr. Act July 1, 1898, c. 541, § 1, subd. 11, 30 Stat. 544, provides that "debt" shall include any debt, demand, or claim provable in bankruptcy; section 4 declares that any "person" who "owes debts," except a corporation, shall be entitled to the benefits of the act as a voluntary bankrupt; and section 63 declares that debts shall be a fixed liability, absolutely owing at the time of the filing of the petition, etc. Held, that the words "owes debts" mean an obligation for which a debtor is legally liable, and hence the bankruptcy act includes an infant, where he owes debts for which his property is legally chargeable. In re Walrath, 175 Fed. 243, 244.

Inhabitant

An inhabitant of the province of Benguet, in the Philippine Islands, was a "person," within Organic Act July 1, 1902, c. 1369, providing that no laws shall be enacted in the Islands which shall deprive any "person" of life, liberty, or property without due process of law, or deny to any person therein the equal protection of the laws. Carino v. Insular Government of Philippine Islands, 29 Sup. Ct. 334, 336, 212 U. S. 449, 53 L. Ed. 594.

Lunatic

Under the bankruptcy act providing that any natural person may be adjudged an involuntary bankrupt, the word "person" does not include a lunatic. In re Kehler, 153 Fed. 235, 237.

Marshal

Where defendant used loud and offensive language in a conversation with a village marshal, as one of a crowd engaged in disturbing the peace, and the marshal neglected to restrain defendant or preserve order, he was not a "person" whose peace could be disturbed, within a village ordinance providing that, if any person shall willfully disturb the peace of any other person by loud and unusual noise, loud and offensive conversation, etc., he shall be adjudged guilty of a misdemeanor. Village of Salem v. Coffey, 88 S. W. 772, 113 Mo. App. 675.

Nonresident

"In the statutes authorizing issuance of garnishment on the application of any 'person,' the word 'person' has been held to include all individuals, nonresidents as well as residents, corporations, and sovereignties." Disconto Gesellschaft v. Umbrelt, 106 N. W. 821, 828, 127 Wis. 651, 15 L. R. A. (N. S.) 1045, 115 Am. St. Rep. 1063 (dissenting opinion by Cassoday, C. J.).

The use of the word "person," in Laws 1905, p. 126, c. 105, amending Rev. St. 1898, c. 2948, by adding the provision that if there be none of such persons in the state, and the defendant corporation has or holds itself out as having an office or place of business in the state, or does business, then service may be made upon the person doing such business or in charge of such office or place of business, the word "person" shows that the Legislature intended to reach a class not covered by the word "agents" used elsewhere in the section, but it is not broad enough to include one merely temporarily in the state, to whom though not connected with the business, was intrusted for collection a bill due a foreign corporation. Honorine Min. & Mill. Co. v. Tellerday Steel Pipe & Tank Co., 88 Pac. 9, 11, 31 Utah, 326.

Officer of corporation

The president of a corporation is a "person," within Comp. Laws. § 4804, declaring that any person, agent, manager, or clerk of a corporation, with whom any money shall be deposited or intrusted, who shall appropriate it to his own use, shall be guilty of embezzlement. State v. Weber, 103 Pac. 411, 412, 31 Nev. 385.

Bankr. Act July 1, 1898, c. 541, § 1, cl. 7, 30 Stat. 544, provides that the term "court"

shall include a referee, and clause 19 declares that the word "persons" includes corporations and officers. By section 2, cl. 7, bankruptcy courts are invested with such jurisdiction in law and in equity as will enable them to exercise original jurisdiction in bankruptcy proceedings to cause the estates of bankrupts to be collected, reduced to money and distributed, and to determine controversies in relation thereto, except as otherwise provided, and section 23, par. "a," confers jurisdiction on the United States Circuit Courts in certain circumstances over controversies between trustees and adverse claimants concerning property claimed by the trustee, except as to proceedings in bankruptcy, jurisdiction over which rests exclusively in bankruptcy courts, and by paragraph "b" suits brought by the trustee, except those to recover property under certain specified sections of the act, can be brought in the bankruptcy court only by consent of the proposed defendant. Held, that a referee in bankruptcy had jurisdiction of a proceeding to compel the officers of a corporation to pay over the proceeds of stock sales alleged to belong to the corporation, and also to pay an amount assessed against them for unpaid shares. In re Kornit Mfg. Co. 192 Fed. 392, 394.

Partnership, firm, company, society, joint-stock company, or association

A "person" includes a joint-stock company. Cole v. Manson, 85 N. Y. Supp. 1011. 42 Misc. Rep. 149.

A partnership is an entity distinct from that of its members, and is recognized in law as a "person." Clay, Robinson & Co. v. Douglas County, 120 N. W. 548, 549, 88 Neb. 363, Ann. Cas. 1912B, 756.

A partnership cannot sue, for it is not a natural or artificial "person." Phillips v. Holmes, 51 South. 625, 626, 165 Ala. 250.

A partnership is a "person" in the sense in which that term is used in the federal bankruptcy act (Act Cong. July 1, 1898, c. 541. § 1, subd. 15, 30 Stat. 544). In re Everybody's Grocery & Meat Market, 173 Fed. 492.

Laws 1892, p. 1487, c. 677, § 5, defines the term "person" to include a corporation or joint association, as well as a natural person. People v. Taylor, 85 N. E. 759, 760. 192 N. Y. 398.

The word "person" or "persons" shall be held to include firms, companies, and associations. Revenue Law (Acts 1898, No. 170, p. 346, § 91). National Fire Ins. Co. v. Board of Assessors, 46 South. 117, 118, 121 La. 10\, 126 Am. St. Rep. 313; General Electric Co. v. Board of Assessors, 46 South. 122, 123, 121 La. 116.

The word "person," as provided by Ky. St. § 457, may extend and be applied to bodies politic and corporate, societies, communities, and the public generally, as well as individuals, persons, and joint-stock com-panics. Commonwealth v. Adams Exp. Co., 97 S. W. 386, 387, 23 Ky. 720.

The word "person," as used in the statutes relating to railroad commissioners, includes partnerships or joint-stock companies. Gen. St. 1901, § 5997. Kansas City, Outer Belt & Electric R. Co. v. Board of Railroad Com'rs, 84 Pac. 755, 756, 73 Kan. 168.

Under Const. art. 9, § 18, giving the Corporation Commission power to regulate all transmission companies doing business in the state in all matters relating to the performance of their public duties and their charges therefor, and section 34, providing that the term "transmission company" shall include any company or other person holding or operating for hire any telegraph or telephone line, and that the term "person" shall include individuals, partnerships, and corporations, the Corporation Commission has supervision of a telephone company owned solely by an individual and operated for hire in all matters relating to the performance of its public duties and charges. Hine v. Wadlington, 109 Pac. 301, 26 Okl. 389.

Laws 1901, p. 19, c. 3, making it unlawful to permit minors in saloons, etc., provides (section 7) that the word "person," as used in the act, shall be deemed to mean firm or corporation, as well as natural person, and the person managing the business of such firm or corporation shall be liable to the penalties prescribed by this act. Territory v. Church, 91 Pac. 720, 721, 14 N. M. 226.

While it is true that section 59 of the Bankrupt Act contains the only provision of the act expressly defining who may file a petition to have a debtor adjudged an involuntary bankrupt, and that that provision is confined to creditors, and section 5, read with section 59, seems to confine the right to creditors, yet section 4a declares that any "person" owing debts, except a corporation, shall be entitled to the benefit of this act as a voluntary bankrupt, and section 1 declares that the word "persons," unless inconsistent with the context, shall include partnerships. In re J. M. Ceballos & Co., 161 Fed. 445, 448.

An unincorporated association is not a "person," and has not the power to sue or be sued; but when it has been organized and conducted for profit it will be treated as a partnership, and its members held liable as partners. Slaughter v. American Baptist Publication Society (Tex.) 150 S. W. 224, 226.

The word "person," in section 2, art. 2, of the general revenue act approved March 10, 1909, providing that "a person moving into this state from another state between March 1st and September 1st shall list his personal property acquiring an actual situs therein before September 1st and the same shall be assessed and placed upon the tax roll and the taxes thereon collected, etc.," includes a firm; and where a firm moves in-

to the state between March 1st and September 1st, moving personal property into the state that acquires a situs therein before September 1st, said property shall be assessed and taxes thereon collected for the current year, notwithstanding one member of the firm was a resident of the state before the 1st day of March, and the other member was, and has been at all times, a resident of another state. Bivins & Carroll v. Bird, 121 Pac. 1080, 1081, 31 Okl. 286.

Under the bankruptcy act of July 1, 1898, a partnership is insolvent if the partnership property is insufficient to pay the firm debts, because it is a "person" (section 1 [19], c. 541, 30 Stat. 545), because any "person" is insolvent under that act whose property is insufficient to pay its debts (section 1 [15], c. 541, 30 Stat. 544), and the only property a partnership has or can apply to its debts is the firm property, and the only debts it owes are the firm debts. In re Bertenshaw, 157 Fed. 363, 368, 85 C. C. A. 61, 17 L. R. A. (N. S.) 886, 13 Ann. Cas. 986.

Neither the judicial recognition by the courts of a state of the partnership entity, nor the provisions of the bankruptcy act, which define a partnership to be a "person" within the meaning of the act, and authorize it to be adjudged a bankrupt (Bankr. Act July 1, 1898, c. 541, §§ 1a [19], 5a, 30 Stat. 544, 547), work a change of the established rule fixing the substantive rights of creditors respectively, of the partnership and of its individual members. In re Telfer, 184 Fed. 224, 226, 106 C. C. A. 366.

Pregnant woman

Laws Del. vol. 17, p. 523, c. 226, § 2 (Rev. Code 1852, amended in 1893, p. 930), makes it a crime for any person to administer to or advise any pregnant woman with intent to procure a miscarriage, or to "aid, assist, or counsel any person so intending to procure a miscarriage." Held, that the word "person," in the quoted clause, means some person other than the pregnant woman, and an indictment under such clause, charging defendants with having counseled a pregnant woman who was intending to procure her own miscarriage, is bad. State v. Parm (Del.) 60 Atl. 977, 978, 5 Pennewill, 556.

Private corporation

The words "person" or "persons" includes corporations. In re Charge to Grand Jury, 151 Fed. 834, 845; Cole v. Manson, 85 N. Y. Supp. 1011, 42 Misc. Rep. 149.

A corporation by both the civil and common law is a "person," an artificial person. Davoust v. City of Alameda, 84 Pac. 760, 761, 149 Cal. 69, 5 L. R. A. (N. S.) 536, 9 Ann. Cas. 847.

A corporation is included in the term "person" as used in the statutes. Goldzier v. Central R. Co. of New Jersey, 88 N. Y. Supp. 214, 215, 43 Misc. Rep. 667 (citing private corporations not possessed by individuals or partnerships," a state is a person, and under section 64b (5) is entitled to priority for a debt due it from the estate of a bankrupt which is given priority by its own insolvency law. In re Western Implement Co., 166 Fed. 576, 582.

Laws 1905, p. 370, c. 175, in amendment of Code Civ. Proc. § 1391, authorizing an execution against the wages or salary of the judgment debtor, and making it the duty of any person or corporation, municipal or otherwise, to whom the execution shall be presented, and who shall be indebted to the judgment debtor, to pay over to the officer the amount of the debt, does not authorize the issuance of an execution against the salary of a state officer; the state being neither a person nor a corporation nor a municipal corporation. Osterhoudt v. Keith, 117 N. Y. Supp. 809, 810, 133 App. Div. 83.

The champerty act (1 Rev. St. p. 739 [1st Ed.] p. 2, c. 1, tit. 2, § 147) provides that "every grant of land shall be absolutely void, if at the time of the delivery thereof, such lands shall be in the actual possession of a person claiming under a title adverse to that of the grantor." Section 9 of the statutory construction law (Laws 1892, p. 1487, c. 677) provides that "the term 'person' includes a corporation and a joint-stock association," and when used to designate a party whose property may be the subject of any offense, the term "person" also includes the state. Held, that the state could therefore only be included as a "person" when the statute relates to any of its property which may be the subject of an offense, and hence the champerty act does not apply to the possession of the state, and that, if the forest commission could be regarded as in actual possession for the state, it would not render the statute applicable as it is no more a "person" than is the state. Saranac Land & Timber Co. v. Roberts, 109 N. Y. Supp. 547, 125 App. Div. 333; Id., 88 N. E. 753, 760, 195 N. Y. 303.

Same—United States

The United States is not a "person" within the meaning of Bankr. Act July 1, 1898, c. 541, § 64, 30 Stat. 563. Title Guaranty & Surety Co. v. Guarantee Title & Trust Co., 174 Fed. 385, 387, 98 C. C. A. 603.

Selectmen

Under Gen. St. 1902, § 2067, authorizing persons interested in altering highways to remonstrate against the report of the committee assessing benefits and damages, and empowering the court to order a jury and "grant relief to the person or persons making such application," when construed in connection with section 2070, providing that, if the report of the jury shall not increase the damages allowed or diminish the assessment of benefits, the court shall order the applicant for the jury to pay the costs of the applica-

tion, etc., the court, in proceedings to assess damages and benefits for the change of the grade of a highway, may not order a jury to make a reassessment of damages and benefits on the application of the town by its selectmen; the selectmen not being referred to by the words "person or persons," in the quoted clause. Selectmen of Town of Montville v. Alpha Mills Co., 81 Atl. 1051, 1052, 85 Conn. 1.

Women

A woman is a "person" within the contemplation of Const. U. S. Amend. 14, § 1, and entitled to the equal protection of the laws. Carrithers v. City of Shelbyville, 104 S. W. 744, 745, 126 Ky. 769, 17 L. R. A. (N. S.) 421 (citing Santa Clara County v. Southern Pac. R. Co., 18 Fed. 385).

PERSON AGGRIEVED

See Aggrieved.

PERSON APPEARING OF RECORD AS OWNER

See Owner of Record.

PERSON ARRIVING IN THE UNITED STATES

Tariff Act July 24, 1897, c. 11, § 2, Free List, par. 697, 30 Stat. 202, provides for "personal effects of persons arriving in the United States," with a proviso relating to "residents of the United States returning from abroad." Held, that the first provision is only for immigrants, and that the proviso concerns Americans only. United States v. Bernays, 158 Fed. 792, 794, 86 C. C. A. 52.

PERSON ASSESSED

See, also, Assess.

Assignors in a common-law assignment for the benefit of creditors to the assignee in trust to pay preferred claims including taxes are the "persons assessed" for taxes within Rev. Laws 1902, c. 13, § 32, authorizing a tax collector to collect a tax by action against the "persons assessed," and they are properly made parties defendant in an action for taxes as the persons primarily liable therefor. Boston v. Turner, 87 N. E. 634, 637, 201 Mass. 190 (citing Ricker v. Brook, 29 N. E. 534, 155 Mass. 400).

PERSON AUTHORIZED

See Authorized by Law; Authorized Person.

PERSON BENEFICIALLY INTERESTED

See Beneficially Interested.

PERSON BENEFITED

See Benefit.

PERSON CAUSING DEATH

See Cause (verb).

PERSON CAUSING EXCAVATION

See Cause (verb).

From Stroud's Judicial Dictionary, first edition

PERSON.—*Primâ facie* the word "Person," in a public statute, includes a Corporation as well as a natural person (per Selborne, L. C., *Pharmaceutical Socy.* v. *Lond. & Provincial Supply Assn.*, 49 L. J. Q. B. 736 ; 5 App. Ca. 857 : *Vf.* ss. 2, 19, Interp. Act, 1889).

" The word ' Person ' may very well include both a natural person (a human being), and an artificial person (a corporation). I think that in an Act of Parliament, unless there be something to the contrary, probably, (I would not like to pledge myself to that) it ought to be held to include both. I have equally no doubt that in common talk, in the language of

584   **PER**

men (not speaking technically), a ' Person ' does not include a corporation. Nobody in common talk, if he were asked who is the richest person in London, would answer, The London and North Western Ry. Co. It is plain that in common speech ' Person ' would mean a natural person. In technical language it may include the other, but which meaning it has in any particular Act, must depend on the context subject-matter. I do not think that the presumption that it includes an artificial person,—a Corporation,—(*if the presumption does arise*)—is at all strong. Circumstances, and indeed very slight circumstances, in the context might show which way the word is to be construed in an Act of Parliament. And I am quite clear about this, that whenever you can see the object of the Act requires that ' Person ' shall have the more extended sense or the less extended sense, then you should apply the word in that sense and construe the Act accordingly " (per Ld. Blackburn, Ib.).

The case from which the definitions just given have been taken shows that " Person " as used in ss. 1 and 15, Pharmacy Act, 1868 (31 & 32 V. c. 121) does not include a Corporation.

The Attorney-General, acting *ex officio*, is not a " Person " within the Statute of Limitation, 3 & 4 W. 4, c. 27 ; but an action by him on behalf of the poor of a parish may be statute barred, as these constitute "a class of persons" within s. 1 (*A.-G.* v. *Magdalen Coll.*, 23 L. J. Ch. 844 ; 18 Bea. 223 : *Magdalen Coll.* v. *A.-G.*, 26 L. J. Ch. 620 ; 6 H. L. Ca. 189). The Ecclesiastical Commrs. are "persons" within ss. 1, 2 of the Act just cited, except in cases where they claim (by virtue of s. 57, 3 & 4 V. c. 113) through an Ecclesiastical Corporation (*Ecclesiastical Commrs.* v. *Rowe*, 49 L. J. Q. B. 771 ; 5 App. Ca. 736).

A Corporation is not a " Person " within the Mortmain Act, 9 G. 2, c. 36, s. 1 (*Walker* v. *Richardson*, 6 L. J. Ex. 229 ; 2 M. & W. 882), nor so as to become a Common Informer (*St. Leonards Shoreditch* v. *Franklin*, 47 L. J. C. P. 727 ; 3 C. P. D. 377).

By the Melbourne Harbour Trust Act a " Person " includes a Corporation, and this was held to include Commissioners appointed under the Act (*Union Steamship Co.* v. *Melbourne Harb. Commrs.*, 53 L. J. P. C. 59 ; 50 L. T. 337 ; 9 App. Ca. 365).

So where trustees of a Will had power to grant leases to " any person or persons " they should think fit, Chitty, J., held that this authorized them to grant a lease to a Limited Company (*Re Jeffcock*, 51 L. J. Ch. 507).

So where a Railway Act provided that " any person " acting in pursuance of it should be entitled to Notice of Action, it was held the Company itself was included (*Boyd* v. *Lond. & Croydon Ry.*, 7 L. J. C. P. 241 ; 4 Bing. N. C. 669 ; 6 Sc. 461).

" Person " in s. 20, Trustee Act, 1850, does not mean person beneficially entitled (*Re Dickson*, W. N. (72) 223).

" Persons belonging to a Ship ; " *V.* Belonging.

" Person by whose act, &c.," Nuisance arises ; *V.* By whose Act.

Appendix B

Human Rights Act 1998

1998 CHAPTER 42

Rights and Freedoms

Article 2 Right to life

1 Everyone's right to life shall be protected by law. No one shall be deprived of his life intentionally save in the execution of a sentence of a court following his conviction of a crime for which this penalty is provided by law.

2 Deprivation of life shall not be regarded as inflicted in contravention of this Article when it results from the use of force which is no more than absolutely necessary:

(a) in defence of any person from unlawful violence;

(b) in order to effect a lawful arrest or to prevent the escape of a person lawfully detained;

(c) in action lawfully taken for the purpose of quelling a riot or insurrection.

Article 3 Prohibition of torture

No one shall be subjected to torture or to inhuman or degrading treatment or punishment.

Article 4 Prohibition of slavery and forced labour

1 No one shall be held in slavery or servitude.

2 No one shall be required to perform forced or compulsory labour.

3 For the purpose of this Article the term "forced or compulsory labour" shall not include:

(a) any work required to be done in the ordinary course of detention imposed according to the provisions of Article 5 of this Convention or during conditional release from such detention;

(b) any service of a military character or, in case of conscientious objectors in countries where they are recognised, service exacted instead of compulsory military service;

(c) any service exacted in case of an emergency or calamity threatening the life or well-being of the community;

(d) any work or service which forms part of normal civic obligations.

Article 5 Right to liberty and security

1 Everyone has the right to liberty and security of person. No one shall be deprived of his liberty save in the following cases and in accordance with a procedure prescribed by law:

(a) the lawful detention of a person after conviction by a competent court;

(b) the lawful arrest or detention of a person for non-compliance with the lawful order of a court or in order to secure the fulfilment of any obligation prescribed by law;

(c) the lawful arrest or detention of a person effected for the purpose of bringing him before the competent legal authority on reasonable suspicion of having committed an offence or when it is reasonably considered necessary to prevent his committing an offence or fleeing after having done so;

(d) the detention of a minor by lawful order for the purpose of educational supervision or his lawful detention for the purpose of bringing him before the competent legal authority;

(e) the lawful detention of persons for the prevention of the spreading of infectious diseases, of persons of unsound mind, alcoholics or drug addicts or vagrants;

(f) the lawful arrest or detention of a person to prevent his effecting an unauthorised entry into the country or of a person against whom action is being taken with a view to deportation or extradition.

2 Everyone who is arrested shall be informed promptly, in a language which he understands, of the reasons for his arrest and of any charge against him.

3 Everyone arrested or detained in accordance with the provisions of paragraph 1(c) of this Article shall be brought promptly before a judge or other officer authorised by law to exercise judicial power and shall be entitled to trial within a reasonable time or to release pending trial. Release may be conditioned by guarantees to appear for trial.

4 Everyone who is deprived of his liberty by arrest or detention shall be entitled to take proceedings by which the lawfulness of his detention shall be decided speedily by a court and his release ordered if the detention is not lawful.

5 Everyone who has been the victim of arrest or detention in contravention of the provisions of this Article shall have an enforceable right to compensation.

Article 6 Right to a fair trial

1 In the determination of his civil rights and obligations or of any criminal charge against him, everyone is entitled to a fair and public hearing within a reasonable time by an independent and impartial tribunal established by law. Judgment shall be pronounced publicly but the press and public may be excluded from all or part of the trial in the interest of morals, public order or national security in a democratic society, where the interests of juveniles or the protection of the private life of the parties so require, or to the extent strictly necessary in the opinion of the court in special circumstances where publicity would prejudice the interests of justice.

2 Everyone charged with a criminal offence shall be presumed innocent until proved guilty according to law.

3 Everyone charged with a criminal offence has the following minimum rights:

(a) to be informed promptly, in a language which he understands and in detail, of the nature and cause of the accusation against him;

(b) to have adequate time and facilities for the preparation of his defence;

(c) to defend himself in person or through legal assistance of his own choosing or, if he has not sufficient means to pay for legal assistance, to be given it free when the interests of justice so require;

(d) to examine or have examined witnesses against him and to obtain the attendance and examination of witnesses on his behalf under the same conditions as witnesses against him;

(e) to have the free assistance of an interpreter if he cannot understand or speak the language used in court.

Article 7 No punishment without law

1 No one shall be held guilty of any criminal offence on account of any act or omission which did not constitute a criminal offence under national or international law at the time when it was committed. Nor shall a heavier penalty be imposed than the one that was applicable at the time the criminal offence was committed.

2 This Article shall not prejudice the trial and punishment of any person for any act or omission which, at the time when it was committed, was criminal according to the general principles of law recognised by civilised nations.

Article 8 Right to respect for private and family life

1 Everyone has the right to respect for his private and family life, his home and his correspondence.

2 There shall be no interference by a public authority with the exercise of this right except such as is in accordance with the law and is necessary in a democratic society in the interests of national security, public safety or the economic well-being of the country, for the prevention of disorder or crime, for the protection of health or morals, or for the protection of the rights and freedoms of others.

Article 9 Freedom of thought, conscience and religion

1 Everyone has the right to freedom of thought, conscience and religion; this right includes freedom to change his religion or belief and freedom, either alone or in community with others and in public or private, to manifest his religion or belief, in worship, teaching, practice and observance.

2 Freedom to manifest one's religion or beliefs shall be subject only to such limitations as are prescribed by law and are necessary in a democratic society in the interests of public safety, for the protection of public order, health or morals, or for the protection of the rights and freedoms of others.

Article 10 Freedom of expression

1 Everyone has the right to freedom of expression. This right shall include freedom to hold opinions and to receive and impart information and ideas without interference by public authority and regardless of frontiers. This Article shall not prevent States from requiring the licensing of broadcasting, television or cinema enterprises.

2 The exercise of these freedoms, since it carries with it duties and responsibilities, may be subject to such formalities, conditions, restrictions or penalties as are prescribed by law and are necessary in a democratic society, in the interests of national security, territorial integrity or public safety, for the prevention of disorder or crime, for the protection of health or morals, for the protection of the reputation or rights of others, for preventing the disclosure of information received in confidence, or for maintaining the authority and impartiality of the judiciary.

Article 11 Freedom of assembly and association

1 Everyone has the right to freedom of peaceful assembly and to freedom of association with others, including the right to form and to join trade unions for the protection of his interests.

2 No restrictions shall be placed on the exercise of these rights other than such as are prescribed by law and are necessary in a democratic society in the interests of national security or public safety, for the prevention of disorder or crime, for the protection of health or morals or for the protection of the rights and freedoms of others. This Article shall not prevent the imposition of lawful restrictions on the exercise of these rights by members of the armed forces, of the police or of the administration of the State.

Article 12 Right to marry

Men and women of marriageable age have the right to marry and to found a family, according to the national laws governing the exercise of this right.

Article 14 Prohibition of discrimination

The enjoyment of the rights and freedoms set forth in this Convention shall be secured without discrimination on any ground such as sex, race, colour, language, religion, political or other opinion, national or social origin, association with a national minority, property, birth or other status.

Article 16 Restrictions on political activity of aliens

Nothing in Articles 10, 11 and 14 shall be regarded as preventing the High Contracting Parties from imposing restrictions on the political activity of aliens.

Article 17 Prohibition of abuse of rights

Nothing in this Convention may be interpreted as implying for any State, group or person any right to engage in any activity or perform any act aimed at the destruction of any of the rights and freedoms set forth herein or at their limitation to a greater extent than is provided for in the Convention.

Article 18 Limitation on use of restrictions on rights

The restrictions permitted under this Convention to the said rights and freedoms shall not be applied for any purpose other than those for which they have been prescribed.

Part II The First Protocol

Article 1 Protection of property

Every natural or legal person is entitled to the peaceful enjoyment of his possessions. No one shall be deprived of his possessions except in the public interest and subject to the conditions provided for by law and by the general principles of international law.

The preceding provisions shall not, however, in any way impair the right of a State to enforce such laws as it deems necessary to control the use of property in accordance with the general interest or to secure the payment of taxes or other contributions or penalties.

Article 2 Right to education

No person shall be denied the right to education. In the exercise of any functions which it assumes in relation to education and to teaching, the State shall respect the right of parents to ensure such education and teaching in conformity with their own religious and philosophical convictions.

Article 3 Right to free elections

The High Contracting Parties undertake to hold free elections at reasonable intervals by secret ballot, under conditions which will ensure the free expression of the opinion of the people in the choice of the legislature.

Part III The Sixth Protocol

Article 1 Abolition of the death penalty

The death penalty shall be abolished. No one shall be condemned to such penalty or executed.

Article 2 Death penalty in time of war

A State may make provision in its law for the death penalty in respect of acts committed in time of war or of imminent threat of war; such penalty shall be applied only in the instances laid down in the law and in accordance with its provisions. The State shall communicate to the Secretary General of the Council of Europe the relevant provisions of that law.

CONVENTION FOR PROTECTION OF
HUMAN RIGHTS AND FUNDAMENTAL FREEDOMS

Rome, 4.XI.1950

Text completed by Protocol No. 2 (ETS No. 44) of 6 May 1963 and amended by Protocol No. 3 (ETS No. 45) of 6 May 1963, Protocol No. 5 (ETS No. 55) of 20 January 1966 and Protocol No. 8 (ETS No. 118) of 19 March 1985

The governments signatory hereto, being members of the Council of Europe,

Considering the Universal Declaration of Human Rights proclaimed by the General Assembly of the United Nations on 10th December 1948;

Considering that this Declaration aims at securing the universal and effective recognition and observance of the Rights therein declared;

Considering that the aim of the Council of Europe is the achievement of greater unity between its members and that one of the methods by which that aim is to be pursued is the maintenance and further realisation of human rights and fundamental freedoms;

Reaffirming their profound belief in those fundamental freedoms which are the foundation of justice and peace in the world and are best maintained on the one hand by an effective political democracy and on the other by a common understanding and observance of the human rights upon which they depend;

Being resolved, as the governments of European countries which are like-minded and have a common heritage of political traditions, ideals, freedom and the rule of law, to take the first steps for the collective enforcement of certain of the rights stated in the Universal Declaration,

Have agreed as follows:

Article 1

The High Contracting Parties shall secure to everyone within their jurisdiction the rights and freedoms defined in Section I of this Convention.

SECTION I

Article 2

1. Everyone's right to life shall be protected by law. No one shall be deprived of his life intentionally save in the execution of a sentence of a court following his conviction of a crime for which this penalty is provided by law.
2. Deprivation of life shall not be regarded as inflicted in contravention of this article when it results from the use of force which is no more than absolutely necessary:

a in defence of any person from unlawful violence;

b in order to effect a lawful arrest or to prevent the escape of a person lawfully detained;

c in action lawfully taken for the purpose of quelling a riot or insurrection.

Article 3

No one shall be subjected to torture or to inhuman or degrading treatment or punishment.

Article 4

1. No one shall be held in slavery or servitude.
2. No one shall be required to perform forced or compulsory labour.
3. For the purpose of this article the term "forced or compulsory labour" shall not include:

a any work required to be done in the ordinary course of detention imposed according to the provisions of Article 5 of this Convention or during conditional release from such detention;

b any service of a military character or, in case of conscientious objectors in countries where they are recognised, service exacted instead of compulsory military service;

c any service exacted in case of an emergency or calamity threatening the life or well-being of the community;

d any work or service which forms part of normal civic obligations.

Article 5

1. Everyone has the right to liberty and security of person. No one shall be deprived of his liberty save in the following cases and in accordance with a procedure prescribed by law:

   a the lawful detention of a person after conviction by a competent court;

   b the lawful arrest or detention of a person for non-compliance with the lawful order of a court or in order to secure the fulfilment of any obligation prescribed by law;

   c the lawful arrest or detention of a person effected for the purpose of bringing him before the competent legal authority on reasonable suspicion of having committed an offence or when it is reasonably considered necessary to prevent his committing an offence or fleeing after having done so;

   d the detention of a minor by lawful order for the purpose of educational supervision or his lawful detention for the purpose of bringing him before the competent legal authority;

   e the lawful detention of persons for the prevention of the spreading of infectious diseases, of persons of unsound mind, alcoholics or drug addicts or vagrants;

   f the lawful arrest or detention of a person to prevent his effecting an unauthorised entry into the country or of a person against whom action is being taken with a view to deportation or extradition.

2. Everyone who is arrested shall be informed promptly, in a language which he understands, of the reasons for his arrest and of any charge against him.
3. Everyone arrested or detained in accordance with the provisions of paragraph 1.c of this article shall be brought promptly before a judge or other officer authorised by law to exercise judicial power and shall be entitled to trial within a reasonable time or to release pending trial. Release may be conditioned by guarantees to appear for trial.
4. Everyone who is deprived of his liberty by arrest or detention shall be entitled to take proceedings by which the lawfulness of his detention shall be decided speedily by a court and his release ordered if the detention is not lawful.
5. Everyone who has been the victim of arrest or detention in contravention of the

provisions of this article shall have an enforceable right to compensation.

Article 6

1. In the determination of his civil rights and obligations or of any criminal charge against him, everyone is entitled to a fair and public hearing within a reasonable time by an independent and impartial tribunal established by law. Judgment shall be pronounced publicly but the press and public may be excluded from all or part of the trial in the interests of morals, public order or national security in a democratic society, where the interests of juveniles or the protection of the private life of the parties so require, or to the extent strictly necessary in the opinion of the court in special circumstances where publicity would prejudice the interests of justice.
2. Everyone charged with a criminal offence shall be presumed innocent until proved guilty according to law.
3. Everyone charged with a criminal offence has the following minimum rights:

a to be informed promptly, in a language which he understands and in detail, of the nature and cause of the accusation against him;

b to have adequate time and facilities for the preparation of his defence;

c to defend himself in person or through legal assistance of his own choosing or, if he has not sufficient means to pay for legal assistance, to be given it free when the interests of justice so require;

d to examine or have examined witnesses against him and to obtain the attendance and examination of witnesses on his behalf under the same conditions as witnesses against him;

e to have the free assistance of an interpreter if he cannot understand or speak the language used in court.

Article 7

1. No one shall be held guilty of any criminal offence on account of any act or omission which did not constitute a criminal offence under national or international law at the time when it was committed. Nor shall a heavier penalty be imposed than the one that was applicable at the time the criminal offence was committed.
2. This article shall not prejudice the trial and punishment of any person for any act or omission which, at the time when it was committed, was criminal according to

the general principles of law recognised by civilised nations.

Article 8

1. Everyone has the right to respect for his private and family life, his home and his correspondence.
2. There shall be no interference by a public authority with the exercise of this right except such as is in accordance with the law and is necessary in a democratic society in the interests of national security, public safety or the economic well-being of the country, for the prevention of disorder or crime, for the protection of health or morals, or for the protection of the rights and freedoms of others.

Article 9

1. Everyone has the right to freedom of thought, conscience and religion; this right includes freedom to change his religion or belief and freedom, either alone or in community with others and in public or private, to manifest his religion or belief, in worship, teaching, practice and observance.
2. Freedom to manifest one's religion or beliefs shall be subject only to such limitations as are prescribed by law and are necessary in a democratic society in the interests of public safety, for the protection of public order, health or morals, or for the protection of the rights and freedoms of others.

Article 10

1. Everyone has the right to freedom of expression. This right shall include freedom to hold opinions and to receive and impart information and ideas without interference by public authority and regardless of frontiers. This article shall not prevent States from requiring the licensing of broadcasting, television or cinema enterprises.
2. The exercise of these freedoms, since it carries with it duties and responsibilities, may be subject to such formalities, conditions, restrictions or penalties as are prescribed by law and are necessary in a democratic society, in the interests of national security, territorial integrity or public safety, for the prevention of disorder or crime, for the protection of health or morals, for the protection of the reputation or rights of others, for preventing the disclosure of information received in confidence, or for maintaining the authority and impartiality of the judiciary.

Article 11

1. Everyone has the right to freedom of peaceful assembly and to freedom of association with others, including the right to form and to join trade unions for the

protection of his interests.

2. No restrictions shall be placed on the exercise of these rights other than such as are prescribed by law and are necessary in a democratic society in the interests of national security or public safety, for the prevention of disorder or crime, for the protection of health or morals or for the protection of the rights and freedoms of others. This article shall not prevent the imposition of lawful restrictions on the exercise of these rights by members of the armed forces, of the police or of the administration of the State.

Article 12

Men and women of marriageable age have the right to marry and to found a family, according to the national laws governing the exercise of this right.

Article 13

Everyone whose rights and freedoms as set forth in this Convention are violated shall have an effective remedy before a national authority notwithstanding that the violation has been committed by persons acting in an official capacity.

Article 14

The enjoyment of the rights and freedoms set forth in this Convention shall be secured without discrimination on any ground such as sex, race, colour, language, religion, political or other opinion, national or social origin, association with a national minority, property, birth or other status.

Article 15

1. In time of war or other public emergency threatening the life of the nation any High Contracting Party may take measures derogating from its obligations under this Convention to the extent strictly required by the exigencies of the situation, provided that such measures are not inconsistent with its other obligations under international law.

2. No derogation from Article 2, except in respect of deaths resulting from lawful acts of war, or from Articles 3, 4 (paragraph 1) and 7 shall be made under this provision.

3. Any High Contracting Party availing itself of this right of derogation shall keep the Secretary General of the Council of Europe fully informed of the measures which it has taken and the reasons therefor. It shall also inform the Secretary General of the Council of Europe when such measures have ceased to operate and the provisions of the Convention are again being fully executed.

Article 16

Nothing in Articles 10, 11 and 14 shall be regarded as preventing the High Contracting Parties from imposing restrictions on the political activity of aliens.

Article 17

Nothing in this Convention may be interpreted as implying for any State, group or person any right to engage in any activity or perform any act aimed at the destruction of any of the rights and freedoms set forth herein or at their limitation to a greater extent than is provided for in the Convention.

Article 18

The restrictions permitted under this Convention to the said rights and freedoms shall not be applied for any purpose other than those for which they have been prescribed.

Universal Declaration of Human Rights

PREAMBLE

Whereas recognition of the inherent dignity and of the equal and inalienable rights of all members of the human family is the foundation of freedom, justice and peace in the world,

Whereas disregard and contempt for human rights have resulted in barbarous acts which have outraged the conscience of mankind, and the advent of a world in which human beings shall enjoy freedom of speech and belief and freedom from fear and want has been proclaimed as the highest aspiration of the common people,

Whereas it is essential, if man is not to be compelled to have recourse, as a last resort, to rebellion against tyranny and oppression, that human rights should be protected by the rule of law,

Whereas it is essential to promote the development of friendly relations between nations,

Whereas the peoples of the United Nations have in the Charter reaffirmed their faith in fundamental human rights, in the dignity and worth of the human person and in the equal rights of men and women and have determined to promote social progress and better standards of life in larger freedom,

Whereas Member States have pledged themselves to achieve, in co-operation with the United Nations, the promotion of universal respect for and observance of human rights and fundamental freedoms,

Whereas a common understanding of these rights and freedoms is of the greatest importance for the full realization of this pledge,

Now, Therefore THE GENERAL ASSEMBLY proclaims THIS UNIVERSAL DECLARATION OF HUMAN RIGHTS as a common standard of achievement for all peoples and all nations, to the end that every individual and every organ of society, keeping this Declaration constantly in mind, shall strive by teaching and education to promote respect for these rights and freedoms and by progressive measures, national and international, to secure their universal and effective recognition and observance, both among the peoples of Member States themselves and among the peoples of territories under their jurisdiction.

^ Top

Article 1.

- All human beings are born free and equal in dignity and rights. They are endowed with reason and conscience and should act towards one another in a spirit of brotherhood.

^ Top

Article 2.

- Everyone is entitled to all the rights and freedoms set forth in this Declaration, without distinction of any kind, such as race, colour, sex, language, religion, political or other opinion, national or social origin, property, birth or other status. Furthermore, no distinction shall be made on the basis of the political, jurisdictional or international status of the country or territory to which a person belongs, whether it be independent, trust, non-self-governing or under any other limitation of sovereignty.

^ Top

Article 3.

- Everyone has the right to life, liberty and security of person.

^ Top

Article 4.

- No one shall be held in slavery or servitude; slavery and the slave trade shall be prohibited in all their forms.

^ Top

Article 5.

- No one shall be subjected to torture or to cruel, inhuman or degrading treatment or punishment.

^ Top

Article 6.

- Everyone has the right to recognition everywhere as a person before the law.

^ Top

Article 7.

- All are equal before the law and are entitled without any discrimination to equal protection of the law. All are entitled to equal protection against any discrimination in violation of this Declaration and against any incitement to such discrimination.

^ Top

Article 8.

- Everyone has the right to an effective remedy by the competent national tribunals for acts violating the fundamental rights granted him by the constitution or by law.

^ Top

Article 9.

- No one shall be subjected to arbitrary arrest, detention or exile.

^ Top

Article 10.

- Everyone is entitled in full equality to a fair and public hearing by an independent and impartial tribunal, in the determination of his rights and obligations and of any criminal charge against him.

^ Top

Article 11.

- (1) Everyone charged with a penal offence has the right to be presumed innocent until proved guilty according to law in a public trial at which he has had all the guarantees necessary for his defence.
- (2) No one shall be held guilty of any penal offence on account of any act or omission which did not constitute a penal offence, under national or international law, at the time when it was committed. Nor shall a heavier penalty be imposed than the one that was applicable at the time the penal offence was committed.

^ Top

Article 12.

- No one shall be subjected to arbitrary interference with his privacy, family, home or correspondence, nor to attacks upon his honour and reputation. Everyone has the right to the protection of the law against such interference or attacks.

^ Top

Article 13.

- (1) Everyone has the right to freedom of movement and residence within the borders of each state.
- (2) Everyone has the right to leave any country, including his own, and to return to his country.

^ Top

Article 14.

- (1) Everyone has the right to seek and to enjoy in other countries asylum from persecution.
- (2) This right may not be invoked in the case of prosecutions genuinely arising from non-political crimes or from acts contrary to the purposes and principles of the United Nations.

^ Top

Article 15.

- (1) Everyone has the right to a nationality.
- (2) No one shall be arbitrarily deprived of his nationality nor denied the right to change his nationality.

^ Top

Article 16.

- (1) Men and women of full age, without any limitation due to race, nationality or religion, have the right to marry and to found a family. They are entitled to equal rights as to marriage, during marriage and at its dissolution.
- (2) Marriage shall be entered into only with the free and full consent of the intending spouses.
- (3) The family is the natural and fundamental group unit of society and is entitled to protection by society and the State.

Article 17.

- (1) Everyone has the right to own property alone as well as in association with others.
- (2) No one shall be arbitrarily deprived of his property.

Article 18.

- Everyone has the right to freedom of thought, conscience and religion; this right includes freedom to change his religion or belief, and freedom, either alone or in community with others and in public or private, to manifest his religion or belief in teaching, practice, worship and observance.

Article 19.

- Everyone has the right to freedom of opinion and expression; this right includes freedom to hold opinions without interference and to seek, receive and impart information and ideas through any media and regardless of frontiers.

Article 20.

- (1) Everyone has the right to freedom of peaceful assembly and association.
- (2) No one may be compelled to belong to an association.

Article 21.

- (1) Everyone has the right to take part in the government of his country, directly or through freely chosen representatives.
- (2) Everyone has the right of equal access to public service in his country.
- (3) The will of the people shall be the basis of the authority of government; this will shall be expressed in periodic and genuine elections which shall be by universal and equal suffrage and shall be held by secret vote or by equivalent free voting procedures.

Article 22.

- Everyone, as a member of society, has the right to social security and is entitled to realization, through national effort and international co-operation and in accordance with the organization and resources of each State, of the economic, social and cultural rights indispensable for his dignity and the free development of his personality.

^ Top

Article 23.

- (1) Everyone has the right to work, to free choice of employment, to just and favourable conditions of work and to protection against unemployment.
- (2) Everyone, without any discrimination, has the right to equal pay for equal work.
- (3) Everyone who works has the right to just and favourable remuneration ensuring for himself and his family an existence worthy of human dignity, and supplemented, if necessary, by other means of social protection.
- (4) Everyone has the right to form and to join trade unions for the protection of his interests.

^ Top

Article 24.

- Everyone has the right to rest and leisure, including reasonable limitation of working hours and periodic holidays with pay.

^ Top

Article 25.

- (1) Everyone has the right to a standard of living adequate for the health and well-being of himself and of his family, including food, clothing, housing and medical care and necessary social services, and the right to security in the event of unemployment, sickness, disability, widowhood, old age or other lack of livelihood in circumstances beyond his control.
- (2) Motherhood and childhood are entitled to special care and assistance. All children, whether born in or out of wedlock, shall enjoy the same social protection.

^ Top

Article 26.

- (1) Everyone has the right to education. Education shall be free, at least in the elementary and fundamental stages. Elementary education shall be compulsory. Technical and professional education shall be made generally available and higher education shall be equally accessible to all on the basis of merit.
- (2) Education shall be directed to the full development of the human personality and to the strengthening of respect for human rights and fundamental freedoms. It shall promote understanding, tolerance and friendship among all nations, racial or religious groups, and shall further the activities of the United Nations for the maintenance of peace.
- (3) Parents have a prior right to choose the kind of education that shall be given to their children.

^ Top

Article 27.

- (1) Everyone has the right freely to participate in the cultural life of the community, to enjoy the arts and to share in scientific advancement and its benefits.
- (2) Everyone has the right to the protection of the moral and material interests resulting from any scientific, literary or artistic production of which he is the author.

^ Top

Article 28.

- Everyone is entitled to a social and international order in which the rights and freedoms set forth in this Declaration can be fully realized.

^ Top

Article 29.

- (1) Everyone has duties to the community in which alone the free and full development of his personality is possible.
- (2) In the exercise of his rights and freedoms, everyone shall be subject only to such limitations as are determined by law solely for the purpose of securing due recognition and respect for the rights and freedoms of others and of meeting the just requirements of morality, public order and the general welfare in a democratic society.

- (3) These rights and freedoms may in no case be exercised contrary to the purposes and principles of the United Nations.

^ Top

Article 30.

- Nothing in this Declaration may be interpreted as implying for any State, group or person any right to engage in any activity or to perform any act aimed at the destruction of any of the rights and freedoms set forth herein.

Interpretation Act 1978

CHAPTER 30

ARRANGEMENT OF SECTIONS

ELIZABETH II

Interpretation Act 1978

1978 CHAPTER 30

An Act to consolidate the Interpretation Act 1889 and certain other enactments relating to the construction and operation of Acts of Parliament and other instruments, with amendments to give effect to recommendations of the Law Commission and the Scottish Law Commission. [20th July 1978]

B E IT ENACTED by the Queen's most Excellent Majesty, by and with the advice and consent of the Lords Spiritual and Temporal, and Commons, in this present Parliament assembled, and by the authority of the same, as follows:—

General provisions as to enactment and operation

1. Every section of an Act takes effect as a substantive enactment without introductory words.

Words of enactment.

2. Any Act may be amended or repealed in the Session of Parliament in which it is passed.

Amendment or repeal in same Session.

3. Every Act is a public Act to be judicially noticed as such, unless the contrary is expressly provided by the Act.

Judicial notice.

4. An Act or provision of an Act comes into force—

   (a) where provision is made for it to come into force on a particular day, at the beginning of that day ;

   (b) where no provision is made for its coming into force, at the beginning of the day on which the Act receives the Royal Assent.

Time of commencement.

B

Interpretation and construction

Definitions.

5. In any Act, unless the contrary intention appears, words and expressions listed in Schedule 1 to this Act are to be construed according to that Schedule.

Gender and number.

6. In any Act, unless the contrary intention appears,—

(a) words importing the masculine gender include the feminine ;

(b) words importing the feminine gender include the masculine ;

(c) words in the singular include the plural and words in the plural include the singular.

References to service by post.

7. Where an Act authorises or requires any document to be served by post (whether the expression "serve" or the expression "give" or "send" or any other expression is used) then, unless the contrary intention appears, the service is deemed to be effected by properly addressing, pre-paying and posting a letter containing the document and, unless the contrary is proved, to have been effected at the time at which the letter would be delivered in the ordinary course of post.

References to distance.

8. In the measurement of any distance for the purposes of an Act, that distance shall, unless the contrary intention appears, be measured in a straight line on a horizontal plane.

References to time of day. 1972 c. 6.

9. Subject to section 3 of the Summer Time Act 1972 (construction of references to points of time during the period of summer time), whenever an expression of time occurs in an Act, the time referred to shall, unless it is otherwise specifically stated, be held to be Greenwich mean time.

References to the Sovereign.

10. In any Act a reference to the Sovereign reigning at the time of the passing of the Act is to be construed, unless the contrary intention appears, as a reference to the Sovereign for the time being.

Construction of subordinate legislation.

11. Where an Act confers power to make subordinate legislation, expressions used in that legislation have, unless the contrary intention appears, the meaning which they bear in the Act.

Statutory powers and duties

Continuity of powers and duties.

12.—(1) Where an Act confers a power or imposes a duty it is implied, unless the contrary intention appears, that the power may be exercised, or the duty is to be performed, from time to time as occasion requires.

(2) Where an Act confers a power or imposes a duty on the holder of an office as such, it is implied, unless the contrary intention appears, that the power may be exercised, or the duty is to be performed, by the holder for the time being of the office.

13. Where an Act which (or any provision of which) does not come into force immediately on its passing confers power to make subordinate legislation, or to make appointments, give notices, prescribe forms or do any other thing for the purposes of the Act, then, unless the contrary intention appears, the power may be exercised, and any instrument made thereunder may be made so as to come into force, at any time after the passing of the Act so far as may be necessary or expedient for the purpose— *Anticipatory exercise of powers.*

> (a) of bringing the Act or any provision of the Act into force ; or
>
> (b) of giving full effect to the Act or any such provision at or after the time when it comes into force.

14. Where an Act confers power to make— *Implied power to amend.*

> (a) rules, regulations or byelaws ; or
>
> (b) Orders in Council, orders or other subordinate legislation to be made by statutory instrument,

it implies, unless the contrary intention appears, a power, exercisable in the same manner and subject to the same conditions or limitations, to revoke, amend or re-enact any instrument made under the power.

Repealing enactments

15. Where an Act repeals a repealing enactment, the repeal does not revive any enactment previously repealed unless words are added reviving it. *Repeal of repeal.*

16.—(1) Without prejudice to section 15, where an Act repeals an enactment, the repeal does not, unless the contrary intention appears,— *General savings.*

> (a) revive anything not in force or existing at the time at which the repeal takes effect ;
>
> (b) affect the previous operation of the enactment repealed or anything duly done or suffered under that enactment ;
>
> (c) affect any right, privilege, obligation or liability acquired, accrued or incurred under that enactment ;
>
> (d) affect any penalty, forfeiture or punishment incurred in respect of any offence committed against that enactment ;

(e) affect any investigation, legal proceeding or remedy in respect of any such right, privilege, obligation, liability, penalty, forfeiture or punishment;

and any such investigation, legal proceeding or remedy may be instituted, continued or enforced, and any such penalty, forfeiture or punishment may be imposed, as if the repealing Act had not been passed.

(2) This section applies to the expiry of a temporary enactment as if it were repealed by an Act.

Repeal and re-enactment.

17.—(1) Where an Act repeals a previous enactment and substitutes provisions for the enactment repealed, the repealed enactment remains in force until the substituted provisions come into force.

(2) Where an Act repeals and re-enacts, with or without modification, a previous enactment then, unless the contrary intention appears,—

(a) any reference in any other enactment to the enactment so repealed shall be construed as a reference to the provision re-enacted;

(b) in so far as any subordinate legislation made or other thing done under the enactment so repealed, or having effect as if so made or done, could have been made or done under the provision re-enacted, it shall have effect as if made or done under that provision.

Miscellaneous

Duplicated offences.

18. Where an act or omission constitutes an offence under two or more Acts, or both under an Act and at common law, the offender shall, unless the contrary intention appears, be liable to be prosecuted and punished under either or any of those Acts or at common law, but shall not be liable to be punished more than once for the same offence.

Citation of other Acts.

19.—(1) Where an Act cites another Act by year, statute, session or chapter, or a section or other portion of another Act by number or letter, the reference shall, unless the contrary intention appears, be read as referring—

(a) in the case of Acts included in any revised edition of the statutes printed by authority, to that edition;

(b) in the case of Acts not so included but included in the edition prepared under the direction of the Record Commission, to that edition;

(c) in any other case, to the Acts printed by the Queen's Printer, or under the superintendence or authority of Her Majesty's Stationery Office.

(2) An Act may continue to be cited by the short title authorised by any enactment notwithstanding the repeal of that enactment.

20.—(1) Where an Act describes or cites a portion of an enactment by referring to words, sections or other parts from or to which (or from and to which) the portion extends, the portion described or cited includes the words, sections or other parts referred to unless the contrary intention appears.

References to other enactments.

(2) Where an Act refers to an enactment, the reference, unless the contrary intention appears, is a reference to that enactment as amended, and includes a reference thereto as extended or applied, by or under any other enactment, including any other provision of that Act.

Supplementary

21.—(1) In this Act " Act " includes a local and personal or private Act; and "subordinate legislation" means Orders in Council, orders, rules, regulations, schemes, warrants, byelaws and other instruments made or to be made under any Act.

Interpretation etc.

(2) This Act binds the Crown.

22.—(1) This Act applies to itself, to any Act passed after the commencement of this Act and, to the extent specified in Part I of Schedule 2, to Acts passed before the commencement of this Act.

Application to Acts and Measures.

(2) In any of the foregoing provisions of this Act a reference to an Act is a reference to an Act to which that provision applies ; but this does not affect the generality of references to enactments or of the references in section 19(1) to other Acts.

(3) This Act applies to Measures of the General Synod of the Church of England (and, so far as it relates to Acts passed before the commencement of this Act, to Measures of the Church Assembly passed after 28th May 1925) as it applies to Acts.

23.—(1) The provisions of this Act, except sections 1 to 3 and 4(*b*), apply, so far as applicable and unless the contrary intention appears, to subordinate legislation made after the commencement of this Act and, to the extent specified in Part II of Schedule 2, to subordinate legislation made before the commencement of this Act, as they apply to Acts.

Application to other instruments.

(2) In the application of this Act to Acts passed or subordinate legislation made after the commencement of this Act, all references to an enactment include an enactment comprised in subordinate legislation whenever made, and references to the

passing or repeal of an enactment are to be construed accordingly.

(3) Sections 9 and 19(1) also apply to deeds and other instruments and documents as they apply to Acts and subordinate legislation; and in the application of section 17(2)(a) to Acts passed or subordinate legislation made after the commencement of this Act, the reference to any other enactment includes any deed or other instrument or document.

(4) Subsections (1) and (2) of this section do not apply to Orders in Council made under section 5 of the Statutory Instruments Act 1946, section 1(3) of the Northern Ireland (Temporary Provisions) Act 1972 or Schedule 1 to the Northern Ireland Act 1974.

Application to Northern Ireland.

24.—(1) This Act extends to Northern Ireland so far as it applies to Acts or subordinate legislation which so extend.

(2) In the application of this Act to Acts passed or subordinate legislation made after the commencement of this Act, all references to an enactment include an enactment comprised in Northern Ireland legislation whenever passed or made; and in relation to such legislation references to the passing or repeal of an enactment include the making or revocation of an Order in Council.

(3) In the application of section 14 to Acts passed after the commencement of this Act which extend to Northern Ireland, " statutory instrument " includes statutory rule for the purposes of the Statutory Rules Act (Northern Ireland) 1958.

(4) The following definitions contained in Schedule 1, namely those of—

British subject and Commonwealth citizen;

The Communities and related expressions;

The Corporation Tax Acts;

The Income Tax Acts;

The Tax Acts,

apply, unless the contrary intention appears, to Northern Ireland legislation as they apply to Acts.

(5) In this section " Northern Ireland legislation " means—

(a) Acts of the Parliament of Ireland;

(b) Acts of the Parliament of Northern Ireland;

(c) Orders in Council under section 1(3) of the Northern Ireland (Temporary Provisions) Act 1972;

(d) Measures of the Northern Ireland Assembly; and

(e) Orders in Council under Schedule 1 to the Northern 1974 c. 28 Ireland Act 1974.

25.—(1) The enactments described in Schedule 3 are repealed Repeals and to the extent specified in the third column of that Schedule. savings.

(2) Without prejudice to section 17(2)(a), a reference to the Interpretation Act 1889, to any provision of that Act or to any 1889 c. 63. other enactment repealed by this Act, whether occurring in another Act, in subordinate legislation, in Northern Ireland legislation or in any deed or other instrument or document, shall be construed as referring to this Act, or to the corresponding provision of this Act, as it applies to Acts passed at the time of the reference.

(3) The provisions of this Act relating to Acts passed after any particular time do not affect the construction of Acts passed before that time, though continued or amended by Acts passed thereafter.

26. This Act shall come into force on 1st January 1979. Commencement.

27. This Act may be cited as the Interpretation Act 1978. Short title.

SCHEDULES

SCHEDULE 1

WORDS AND EXPRESSIONS DEFINED

Note : The years or dates which follow certain entries in this Schedule are relevant for the purposes of paragraph 4 of Schedule 2 (application to existing enactments).

Definitions

" Associated state " means a territory maintaining a status of 1967 c. 4. association with the United Kingdom in accordance with the West Indies Act 1967. [16th February 1967]

" Bank of England " means, as the context requires, the Governor and Company of the Bank of England or the bank of the Governor and Company of the Bank of England.

" Bank of Ireland " means, as the context requires, the Governor and Company of the Bank of Ireland or the bank of the Governor and Company of the Bank of Ireland.

" British Islands " means the United Kingdom, the Channel Islands and the Isle of Man. [1889]

" British possession " means any part of Her Majesty's dominions outside the United Kingdom ; and where parts of such dominions are under both a central and a local legislature, all parts under the central legislature are deemed, for the purposes of this definition, to be one British possession. [1889]

" British subject " and " Commonwealth citizen " have the same meaning, that is—

1948 c. 56.
    (*a*) a person who under the British Nationality Act 1948 is a citizen of the United Kingdom and Colonies or who under any enactment for the time being in force in a country mentioned in section 1(3) of that Act is a citizen of that country ; and

    (*b*) any other person who has the status of a British subject under that Act or any subsequent enactment.

" Building regulations ", in relation to England and Wales, means 1936 c. 49. regulations made under section 61(1) of the Public Health Act 1936.

" Central funds ", in an enactment providing in relation to England and Wales for the payment of costs out of central funds, means money provided by Parliament.

" Charity Commissioners " means the Charity Commissioners for 1960 c. 58. England and Wales referred to in section 1 of the Charities Act 1960.

" Church Commissioners " means the Commissioners constituted 1947 by the Church Commissioners Measure 1947.
C.A.M. No. 2.

" Colonial legislature ", and " legislature " in relation to a British possession, mean the authority, other than the Parliament of the United Kingdom or Her Majesty in Council, competent to make laws for the possession. [1889]

" Colony " means any part of Her Majesty's dominions outside the British Islands except—

(a) countries having fully responsible status within the Commonwealth ;

(b) territories for whose external relations a country other than the United Kingdom is responsible ;

(c) associated states ;

and where parts of such dominions are under both a central and a local legislature, all parts under the central legislature are deemed for the purposes of this definition to be one colony. [1889]

" Commencement ", in relation to an Act or enactment, means the time when the Act or enactment comes into force.

" Committed for trial " means—

(a) in relation to England and Wales, committed in custody or on bail by a magistrates' court pursuant to section 7 of the Magistrates' Courts Act 1952, or by any judge or other authority having power to do so, with a view to trial before a judge and jury ; [1889]   1952 c. 55.

(b) in relation to Northern Ireland, committed in custody or on bail by a magistrates' court pursuant to section 45 of the Magistrates' Courts Act (Northern Ireland) 1964, or by a court, judge, resident magistrate, justice of the peace or other authority having power to do so, with a view to trial on indictment. [1st January 1979]   1964 c. 21 (N.I.).

" The Communities ", " the Treaties " or " the Community Treaties " and other expressions defined by section 1 of and Schedule 1 to the European Communities Act 1972 have the meanings prescribed by that Act.   1972 c. 68.

" Comptroller and Auditor General " means the Comptroller-General of the receipt and issue of Her Majesty's Exchequer and Auditor-General of Public Accounts appointed in pursuance of the Exchequer and Audit Departments Act 1866.   1866 c. 39.

" Consular officer " has the meaning assigned by Article 1 of the Vienna Convention set out in Schedule 1 to the Consular Relations Act 1968.   1968 c. 18.

" The Corporation Tax Acts " means—

(a) Parts X and XI of the Income and Corporation Taxes Act 1970 ;   1970 c. 10.

(b) all other provisions of that or any other Act relating to corporation tax or to any other matter dealt with in Part X or Part XI of that Act ;

(c) all the provisions of Part IV of the Finance Act 1965 and of any other enactment which, at the passing of the said Act of 1970, formed part of or was to be construed with the Corporation Tax Acts.   1965 c. 25.

Sch. 1

1959 c. 22.

1959 c. 25
(N.I.).

" County court " means—

(a) in relation to England and Wales, a court held for a district under the County Courts Act 1959 ; [1846]

(b) in relation to Northern Ireland, a court held for a division under the County Courts Act (Northern Ireland) 1959. [1889]

" Court of Appeal " means—

(a) in relation to England and Wales, Her Majesty's Court of Appeal in England ;

(b) in relation to Northern Ireland, Her Majesty's Court of Appeal in Northern Ireland.

" Court of summary jurisdiction ", " summary conviction " and " Summary Jurisdiction Acts ", in relation to Northern Ireland, have the same meanings as in Measures of the Northern Ireland Assembly and Acts of the Parliament of Northern Ireland.

" Crown Court " means—

1971 c. 23.

(a) in relation to England and Wales, the Crown Court constituted by section 4 of the Courts Act 1971 ;

1978 c. 23.

(b) in relation to Northern Ireland, the Crown Court constituted by section 4 of the Judicature (Northern Ireland) Act 1978.

1961 c. 55.

" Crown Estate Commissioners " means the Commissioners referred to in secton 1 of the Crown Estate Act 1961.

1972 c. 70.

" England " means, subject to any alteration of boundaries under Part IV of the Local Government Act 1972, the area consisting of the counties established by section 1 of that Act, Greater London and the Isles of Scilly. [1st April 1974].

" Financial year " means, in relation to matters relating to the Consolidated Fund, the National Loans Fund, or moneys provided by Parliament, or to the Exchequer or to central taxes or finance, the twelve months ending with 31st March. [1889]

" Governor-General " includes any person who for the time being has the powers of the Governor-General, and " Governor ", in relation to any British possession, includes the officer for the time being administering the government of that possession. [1889]

" High Court " means—

(a) in relation to England and Wales, Her Majesty's High Court of Justice in England ;

(b) in relation to Northern Ireland, Her Majesty's High Court of Justice in Northern Ireland.

" The Income Tax Acts " means all enactments relating to income tax, including any provisions of the Corporation Tax Acts which relate to income tax.

" Land " includes buildings and other structures, land covered with water, and any estate, interest, easement, servitude or right in or over land. [1st January 1979].

" Lands Clauses Acts " means—   SCH. 1

    (*a*) in relation to England and Wales, the Lands Clauses Con- 1845 c. 18.
solidation Act 1845 and the Lands Clauses Consolidation 1860 c. 106.
Acts Amendment Act 1860, and any Acts for the time being
in force amending those Acts ; [1889]

    (*b*) in relation to Scotland, the Lands Clauses Consolidation 1845 c. 19.
(Scotland) Act 1845 and the Lands Clauses Consolidation 1860 c. 106.
Acts Amendment Act 1860, and any Acts for the time being
in force amending those Acts ; [1889]

    (*c*) in relation to Northern Ireland, the enactments defined as
such by section 46(1) of the Interpretation Act (Northern 1954 c. 53
Ireland) 1954. [1889]   (N.I.).

" Local land charges register ", in relation to England and Wales,
means a register kept pursuant to section 3 of the Local Land 1975 c. 76.
Charges Act 1975, and " the appropriate local land charges register "
has the meaning assigned by section 4 of that Act.

" London borough " means a borough described in Schedule 1 to
the London Government Act 1963, " inner London borough " means 1963 c. 33.
one of the boroughs so described and numbered from 1 to 12 and
" outer London borough " means one of the boroughs so described
and numbered from 13 to 32, subject (in each case) to any alterations
made under Part IV of the Local Government Act 1972.   1972 c. 70.

" Lord Chancellor " means the Lord High Chancellor of Great
Britain.

" Magistrates' court " has the meaning assigned to it—

    (*a*) in relation to England and Wales, by section 124 of the
Magistrates' Courts Act 1952 ;   1952 c. 55.

    (*b*) in relation to Northern Ireland, by section 1 of the Magis- 1964 c. 21
trates' Courts Act (Northern Ireland) 1964.   (N.I.).

" Month " means calendar month. [1850]

" National Debt Commissioners " means the Commissioners for the
Reduction of the National Debt.

" Northern Ireland legislation " has the meaning assigned by
section 24(5) of this Act. [1st January 1979]

" Oath " and " affidavit " include affirmation and declaration, and
" swear " includes affirm and declare.

" Ordnance Map " means a map made under powers conferred
by the Ordnance Survey Act 1841 or the Boundary Survey (Ireland) 1841 c. 30.
Act 1854.   1854 c. 17.

" Parliamentary Election " means the election of a Member to serve
in Parliament for a constituency. [1889]

" Person " includes a body of persons corporate or unincorporate.
[1889]

SCH. 1   " Police area ", " police authority " and other expressions relating to the police have the meaning or effect described—

1964 c. 48.   (a) in relation to England and Wales, by section 62 of the Police Act 1964 ;

1967 c. 77.   (b) in relation to Scotland, by sections 50 and 51(4) of the Police (Scotland) Act 1967.

" The Privy Council " means the Lords and others of Her Majesty's Most Honourable Privy Council.

1956 c. 76.   " Registered medical practitioner " means a fully registered person within the meaning of the Medical Act 1956. [1st January 1979]

" Rules of Court " in relation to any court means rules made by the authority having power to make rules or orders regulating the practice and procedure of that court, and in Scotland includes Acts of Adjournal and Acts of Sederunt ; and the power of the authority to make rules of court (as above defined) includes power to make such rules for the purpose of any Act which directs or authorises anything to be done by rules of court. [1889]

" Secretary of State " means one of Her Majesty's Principal Secretaries of State.

" Sheriff ", in relation to Scotland, includes sheriff principal. [1889]

1835 c. 62.   " Statutory declaration " means a declaration made by virtue of the Statutory Declarations Act 1835.

" Supreme Court " means—

(a) in relation to England and Wales, the Court of Appeal and the High Court together with the Crown Court ;

(b) in relation to Northern Ireland, the Supreme Court of Judicature of Northern Ireland.

1970 c. 10.   " The Tax Acts " means the Income and Corporation Taxes Act 1970 and all other provisions of the Income Tax Acts and the Corporation Tax Acts. [12th March 1970]

" The Treasury " means the Commissioners of Her Majesty's Treasury.

" United Kingdom " means Great Britain and Northern Ireland. [12th April 1927]

1972 c. 70.   " Wales " means, subject to any alteration of boundaries made under Part IV of the Local Government Act 1972, the area consisting of the counties established by section 20 of that Act. [1st April 1974]

1973 c. 37.   " Water authority ", in relation to England and Wales, means an authority established in accordance with section 2 of the Water Act 1973 ; and " water authority area ", in relation to any functions of such an authority, means the area in respect of which the water authority are for the time being to exercise those functions.

" Writing " includes typing, printing, lithography, photography and other modes of representing or reproducing words in a visible form, and expressions referring to writing are construed accordingly.

Construction of certain expressions relating to children SCH. 1

In relation to England and Wales the following expressions and references, namely—

(a) the expression " the parental rights and duties " ;

(b) the expression " legal custody " in relation to a child (as defined in the Children Act 1975) ; and   1975 c. 72.

(c) any reference to the person with whom a child (as so defined) has his home,

are to be construed in accordance with Part IV of that Act. [12th November 1975]

Construction of certain expressions relating to offences

In relation to England and Wales—

(a) " indictable offence " means an offence which, if committed by an adult, is triable on indictment, whether it is exclusively so triable or triable either way ;

(b) " summary offence " means an offence which, if committed by an adult, is triable only summarily ;

(c) " offence triable either way " means an offence which, if committed by an adult, is triable either on indictment or summarily ;

and the terms " indictable ", " summary " and " triable either way ", in their application to offences, are to be construed accordingly.

In the above definitions references to the way or ways in which an offence is triable are to be construed without regard to the effect, if any, of section 23 of the Criminal Law Act 1977 on the mode of 1977 c. 45. trial in a particular case.

SCHEDULE 2   Sections 22, 23.

APPLICATION OF ACT TO EXISTING ENACTMENTS

PART I

ACTS

1. The following provisions of this Act apply to Acts whenever passed : —

Section 6(a) and (c) so far as applicable to enactments relating to offences punishable on indictment or on summary conviction
Section 9
Section 10
Section 11 so far as it relates to subordinate legislation made after the year 1889
Section 18
Section 19(2).

2. The following apply to Acts passed after the year 1850 : —

Section 1
Section 2

Section 3
Section 6(a) and (c) so far as not applicable to such Acts by
  virtue of paragraph 1
Section 15
Section 17(1).

3. The following apply to Acts passed after the year 1889 : —
Section 4
Section 7
Section 8
Section 12
Section 13
Section 14 so far as it relates to rules, regulations or byelaws
Section 16(1)
Section 17(2)(a)
Section 19(1)
Section 20(1).

4.—(1) Subject to the following provisions of this paragraph—

    (a) paragraphs of Schedule 1 at the end of which a year or date
earlier than the commencement of this Act is specified apply,
so far as applicable, to Acts passed on or after the date,
or after the year, so specified ; and

    (b) paragraphs of that Schedule at the end of which no year or
date is specified apply, so far as applicable, to Acts passed
at any time.

(2) The definition of " British Islands ", in its application to Acts
passed after the establishment of the Irish Free State but before
the commencement of this Act, includes the Republic of Ireland.

(3) The definition of " colony ", in its application to an Act passed
at any time before the commencement of this Act, includes—

    (a) any colony within the meaning of section 18(3) of the Inter-
pretation Act 1889 which was excluded, but in relation only
to Acts passed at a later time, by any enactment repealed
by this Act ;

    (b) any country or territory which ceased after that time to be
part of Her Majesty's dominions but subject to a provision
for the continuation of existing law as if it had not so
ceased ;

and paragraph (b) of the definition does not apply.

(4) The definition of " Lord Chancellor " does not apply to Acts
passed before 1st October 1921 in which that expression was used in
relation to Ireland only.

(5) The definition of " person ", so far as it includes bodies
corporate, applies to any provision of an Act whenever passed
relating to an offence punishable on indictment or on summary
conviction.

(6) This paragraph applies to the National Health Service
Reorganisation Act 1973 and the Water Act 1973 as if they were
passed after 1st April 1974.

Interpretation Act 1978 c. 30 15

5. The following definitions shall be treated as included in Schedule 1 for the purposes specified in this paragraph—

(a) in any Act passed before 1st April 1974, a reference to England includes Berwick upon Tweed and Monmouthshire and, in the case of an Act passed before the Welsh Language Act 1967, Wales ;   1967 c. 66.

(b) in any Act passed before the commencement of this Act and after the year 1850, " land " includes messuages, tenements and hereditaments, houses and buildings of any tenure ;

(c) in any Act passed before the commencement of the Criminal Procedure (Scotland) Act 1975, "the Summary Jurisdiction (Scotland) Acts " means Part II of that Act.   1975 c. 21.

PART II

SUBORDINATE LEGISLATION

6. Sections 4(a), 9 and 19(1), and so much of Schedule 1 as defines the following expressions, namely—

British subject and Commonwealth citizen :

England :

Local land charges register and appropriate local land charges register ;

Police area (and related expressions) in relation to Scotland :

United Kingdom ;

Wales,

apply to subordinate legislation made at any time before the commencement of this Act as they apply to Acts passed at that time.

7. The definition in Schedule 1 of " county court ", in relation to England and Wales, applies to Orders in Council made after the year 1846.

SCHEDULE 3

ENACTMENTS REPEALED

Chapter or Number	Short Title	Extent of Repeal
20 Geo. 2. c. 42.	The Wales and Berwick Act 1746.	The whole Act.
33 Geo. 3. c. 13.	The Acts of Parliament (Commencement) Act 1793.	The words from " and to be the date " to the end.
43 & 44 Vict. c. 9.	The Statutes (Definition of Time) Act 1880.	The whole Act.
47 & 48 Vict. c. 62.	The Revenue Act 1884.	In section 14, the second paragraph, that is the words from " Any reference " to " Exchequer and Audit Departments Act 1866 " in the second place where that Act is referred to in the section.
52 & 53 Vict. c. 63.	The Interpretation Act 1889.	The whole Act except paragraphs (4), (5) and (14) of section 13 in their application to Northern Ireland.
53 & 54 Vict. c. 21.	The Inland Revenue Regulation Act 1890.	In section 38(1), the words from " and " to " of this Act ".
59 & 60 Vict. c. 14.	The Short Titles Act 1896.	Section 3.
S.R. & O. 1923 No. 405.	The Irish Free State (Consequential Adaptation of Enactments) Order 1923.	In the Schedule, the entry relating to the Interpretation Act 1889.
15 & 16 Geo. 5. No. 1.	The Interpretation Measure 1925.	Section 1.
17 & 18 Geo. 5. c. 4.	The Royal and Parliamentary Titles Act 1927.	In section 2(2) the words " Act passed and ".
22 & 23 Geo. 5. c. 4.	The Statute of Westminster 1931.	Section 11.
11 & 12 Geo. 6. c. 7.	The Ceylon Independence Act 1947.	Section 4(2).
11 & 12 Geo. 6. c. 56.	The British Nationality Act 1948.	In section 1(2) the words " other enactment or " and the words " passed or ".
15 & 16 Geo. 6 & 1 Eliz. 2. c. 55.	The Magistrates' Courts Act 1952.	In Schedule 5, the amendment of the Interpretation Act 1889.
4 & 5 Eliz. 2. c. 76.	The Medical Act 1956.	Section 52(3).
5 & 6 Eliz. 2. c. 6.	The Ghana Independence Act 1957.	Section 4(1).
8 & 9 Eliz. 2. c. 55.	The Nigeria Indepedence Act 1960.	Section 3(1).
9 & 10 Eliz. 2. c. 16.	The Sierra Leone Independence Act 1961.	Section 3(1).
10 & 11 Eliz. 2. c. 1.	The Tanganyika Independence Act 1961.	Section 3(1).
10 & 11 Eliz. 2. c. 30.	The Northern Ireland Act 1962.	Section 27.